WHAT ARE THEY SAYING ABOUT CATHOLIC ETHICAL METHOD?

What Are They Saying About Catholic Ethical Method?

Todd A. Salzman

PAULIST PRESS
New York/Mahwah, N.J.

Cover design by James F. Brisson

Library of Congress Cataloging-in-Publication Data

Salzman, Todd A.
    What are they saying about Catholic ethical method? / Todd A. Salzman.
       p.   cm.
    Includes bibliographical references and index.
    ISBN 0-8091-4159-0 (alk. paper)
    1. Christian ethics—Catholic authors. 2. Catholic Church—Doctrines.
I. Title.
BJ1249 .S329 2003
241′.042′01—dc21

2003004421

Published by Paulist Press
997 Macarthur Boulevard
Mahwah, New Jersey 07430

www.paulistpress.com

Printed and bound in the
United States of America

Contents

To my wife, Katy,
and our three children,
Ian, Aaron, and Emily

Preface

This book is intended to introduce lay readers to the current debate on method in Catholic moral theology and to attempt to shed new light on that debate for Catholic moral theologians. The two ethical theories that we will investigate are both grounded in the Catholic natural law tradition and are designated as the Basic Goods Theory (BGT), also known as the New Natural Law Theory, and revisionism. Revisionism, as it is used in this text, includes the school known as proportionalism. However, revisionism goes beyond the norm of proportionate reason for determining right or wrong acts and includes a variety of methodological components that form its ethical theory. In analyzing the BGT and revisionism, it is important to recognize their unique historical evolution. The BGT was primarily developed and proposed as a theological ethic through the work of Germain Grisez, especially in the three volumes of his modern manual of moral theology, *The Way of the Lord Jesus.* The philosophical components of this method have been worked out over the years by Grisez in conjunction with John Finnis and Joseph Boyle. While other theologians and philosophers have associated themselves with the BGT, they largely accept both its initial philosophical development and formulation. As a result, the BGT tends to be more univocal than revisionism both in its development of ethical method and its normative conclusions. Revisionism, on the other hand, is a much broader method that originated through the work of European theologians and has spread to the United States. As a result, it is a much more diverse ethical method. The theological perceptions and interpretations of the sources of moral knowledge that constitute the ethical method generally known as revisionism and the normative conclusions reached in applying this method to particular ethical issues are far more diverse than in the BGT. Since there is no single "revisionist method," my development in this text is based on some of the most influential voices in the United States and Europe who have been responsible for laying its foundations and developing it since Vatican II. In no way do I presume to have presented revisionism in its entirety, and I imagine that some revisionist moral theologians may disagree with my choice and presentation of those methodological components that I consider essential to revisionism. Nonetheless, I hope that my investigation will both spark discussion and perhaps even clarify some aspects of the respective ethical methods of revisionism and the BGT, thus facilitating dialogue between them.

I would like to thank my colleague in theology at Creighton University, Dr. Julia Fleming, and Dr. Robert J. Cain and Mrs. Barbara Cain, for their comments and suggestions in reviewing this text. I am also indebted to the Summer Faculty Development Grant provided by Creighton University Graduate School for its generous financial support to facilitate the completion of this work.

Introduction

It would not be too much of an exaggeration to say that, since the 1960s, a schism has developed in Catholic moral theology that has profound implications for the Catholic Church today. The schism separates those theologians known as revisionists and those who have developed a new natural law ethical theory, which we will refer to in this text as the Basic Goods Theory (BGT). The revisionist camp includes the school that is commonly referred to as proportionalism. Revisionism, however, is a broader school that envisions the entire revision of Catholic moral theology, and does not focus exclusively on the normative ethical realm.[1] The BGT includes those who espouse the "new natural law," developed by Germain Grisez, John Finnis, and Joseph Boyle; among others in this group are Russell Shaw and William May. Both schools have attempted to respond to Vatican II's call for a renewal in moral theology, but have done so in very different ways. Whereas the BGT has developed a complex normative ethical theory to explain and justify specific moral norms, including the absolute norms taught by the magisterium, revisionism's theory has sometimes challenged these teachings. These attempts at renewal have been the subject of scholarly, and even sometimes acrimonious, debate between the two schools of thought, as well as the object of official magisterial pronouncements.

Pope John Paul II's encyclical on fundamental moral theology, *Veritatis Splendor* (The Splendor of Truth)[2], both implicitly recognized and confirmed this schism, but by no means resolved it. It recognized the schism by addressing a popular contemporary approach to moral theology known as proportionalism or "teleologism" [sic].[3] Though it clearly condemned this approach to moral theology as mistaken, and at times even utilized the BGT's terminology and reasoning[4] (thereby implicitly suggesting that the BGT is an officially approved ethical theory), it did not settle the academic debate among Catholic moral theologians. It did not do so because the ethical approach that it condemned is not an accurate representation of the revisionist position.[5] What the encyclical did do, however, was to emphasize the need for a clear conceptual understanding of the two predominant interpretations of natural law ethical theory within the Catholic Church.

What is it that fundamentally divides these two ethical theories? What has created such animosity and division not only among theologians but also within the church herself? This work attempts to respond to these questions. In laying the foundations for such an investigation, we will first distinguish between various levels of ethical discourse. We will identify *method* as the level of ethical discourse that justifies our claims to moral truth and the locus of the debate between revisionism and the BGT. We will then look at the *sources* of moral knowledge in the Catholic Christian tradition and see how the emphasis on each of these sources, as well as their prioritization and interpretation, gives rise to fundamentally different ethical theories. Chapter 1 will present an overview of the two theories. Chapters 2, 3, and 4 will provide a more detailed investigation of the sources of moral knowledge and how they function in each theory. We will conclude by suggesting areas of common ground between the two theories as a basis for dialogue.

Status Quaestionis

A famous scholastic aphorism, "Philosophy is the handmaid of theology,"[6] is particularly apropos of our topic, Catholic normative ethical method.[7] Until Vatican II, the manuals of moral theology were *the* authoritative sources of moral theology within Catholicism. These manuals originated in response to the Council of Trent's call for an educated clergy and functioned primarily, if not exclusively, to train seminarians to hear confessions. As a result, they tended to focus on practical considerations rather than on theoretical reflection, philosophical analysis, or methodological discussion or development. The call for the renewal of moral theology, which was already under way prior to the council,[8] was voiced at Vatican II and implicitly challenged the approach of the manualist tradition.

Given the historical context out of which the manuals arose and the purpose for which they were written, it is quite fitting that the call for renewal in moral theology would be proclaimed in the Vatican II document entitled *Optatam Totius* (Decree on Priestly Formation). The frequently cited quotation is taken from paragraph 16 of this document:

> Special attention needs to be given to the development of moral theology. Its scientific exposition should be more thoroughly nourished by scriptural teaching. It should show the nobility of the Christian vocation of the faithful, and their obligation to bring forth fruit in charity for the life of the world.[9]

In this passage, the importance of the renewal of moral theology and the significance of scripture for this renewal are clearly articulated. In a previous paragraph, however, this document asserts, "In the revision of ecclesiastical studies, the first object in view must be a better integration of philosophy and theology" (14). The following paragraph goes on to explain the importance of the dialogue between philosophy and theology in clarifying and coming to a deeper understanding of the "mysteries of salvation" (15). Certainly the call for philosophical integration is expanded to include moral theology as well.

In response to this call, many moral theologians in the post-Vatican II era have consulted the work of philosophers in order to construct what the manuals of moral theology neglected—an explicit normative method. This project has resulted in a concentrated effort among moral theologians to reconstruct Catholic moral theology, although revisionists and those who developed the BGT have done so in different ways. In particular, two issues have attracted a great deal of attention and have sparked debate between these schools. The first issue entails constructing a normative method. (As noted, the manuals were not concerned with developing a solid method or ethical theory.) Much of the focus in the renewal movement has been to formulate a coherent normative method and draw out its logical implications for Christian ethics. Revisionism and the BGT are the two main schools undertaking this methodological reconstruction. Method, especially with regard to the foundation and formulation of norms, is frequently considered the area of renewal in Catholic moral theology; however, *method* itself is rarely defined. What are the parameters of ethical method? Is it concerned primarily with meta-ethics, normative ethics, or moral judgments?[10] Does Christian ethical method differ from philosophical ethical method, and if so, how? Further, what, if anything, does the Catholic tradition contribute to ethical method? To respond to these questions, we must begin our excursion into method by considering philosophical perspectives on ethics in general and method in particular.

Philosophical Division of Ethics

Philosophical ethicists frequently distinguish between three levels of ethical discourse: moral judgments, normative ethics, and meta-ethics.[11] As human beings endowed with reason and the ability to choose, we all make moral judgments on the basis of what we believe is right, obligatory, or good. This is the realm of daily moral decision making, and is technically referred to as the realm of morality. Since moral judgments serve as the source for normative ethics and meta-ethics, it is important to understand clearly a moral judgment and its role and function in ethics. We could posit two types of moral judgments that have different implications for reflections on those judgments: *actual* and *possible* moral judgments. Actual moral judgments are judgments of conscience whereby the moral agent makes a choice to do or not do something, given all the particularities of his situation guided by conscience. For example, I may choose not to pay taxes because that money is used to support and develop military weapons of mass destruction. Possible moral judgments are speculative moral judgments made by an individual on an issue. For example, capital punishment is wrong. Actual moral judgments encompass the full meaning of the human act, both the objective and subjective dimensions. The rightness or wrongness of an act "...must be determined by objective standards...based on the nature of the human person and his acts...."[12] Subjectively, what this act says about the individual's conscience, character, motive, relationships, commitments, beliefs, ideals, values, etc., is a key consideration as well. Elsewhere, I have referred to this holistic description of the human act as "the human act adequately considered."[13] Since actual moral judgments combine the objective and subjective dimensions, they are not the best source for ethical reflection. Actual moral judgments are too particular in the sense that each individual is a unique entity, and therefore each actual judgment that he or she makes is to a certain extent unique to that individual. Normative ethics is concerned with generalizations about human experience in the foundation and formulation of norms. Such particular dimensions of the human act adequately considered are too narrowly focused to form such generalizations. Possible moral judgments, on the other hand, are more conducive to ethical reflection. These judgments suspend the particularity of actual moral judgments and seek to formulate norms that can extrapolate common aspects of human experience in the form of generalizations. As we shall see, the distinction between actual and possible moral judgments is important when analyzing the methods of revisionism and the BGT.

While it is the business of all rational human beings to make moral judgments in light of what a person thinks he or she "ought to do," "is the right thing to do," or "is good to do," it is primarily the work of philosophical and Christian ethics to critically reflect upon, analyze, and develop these moral judgments into a comprehensive, systematic, rational, and generalizable theory. The synopsis and synthesis of possible moral judgments into such a theory is the area of normative ethics and meta-ethics. Normative ethics attempts to answer questions about what is good, right, or obligatory and to formulate laws, rules, norms, or guidelines for the attainment of the values designated within that definition. Normative ethics proposes norms that prohibit or prescribe: (1) actions (e.g., "do not kill"); (2) dispositions, motivations, or types of character (e.g., "respect life"); and (3) actions that entail descriptions of both the act and the motive (e.g., "do not murder").

In his definition of meta-ethics, William Frankena explains that the basic questions of meta-ethics concern the meaning of ethical terms and the justification of ethical and value judgments.[14] The meaning or use of ethical terms is considered under the auspices of semantic questions. For example, what is the meaning of the terms *right* or *good?* Do these terms have any meaning at all? How are these terms used? The realm of meta-ethics that addresses the meaning of ethical terms attempts to respond to these questions. For example, nihilism is "the doctrine that there are no moral facts, no moral truths, and no moral knowledge."[15] Ethical relativism claims that moral truth can only be determined within a particular culture; there is no universal truth.[16] Objectivism claims that there is universal moral truth, and that we can know this truth. The justification of ethical and value judgments is considered under the category of epistemic questions, according to Frankena. For example, if we espouse an objectivist meta-ethic, how can we justify our claims to moral knowledge? It is the epistemic question that Frankena considers primary for meta-ethics.[17] One may legitimately ask whether there is any meaningful distinction between epistemic (justification) and semantic (meaning) questions in ethical theory. The importance of the distinction can be seen when one looks at the relationship between the justification of ethical and value judgments and the meaning of ethical terms, especially in Catholic ethical discourse.

Both revisionism and the BGT espouse an objectivist, natural law meta-ethic. Natural law may be defined as the "participation of the eternal law in the rational creature."[18] Revisionism and the BGT both accept that there is universal moral truth, and that human beings can know this truth through the use of reason. Truth or rectitude concerning general principles of speculative and practical reason is the same for all, and can be known by all through reason.[19] The moral precepts of the natural law proceed from the dictate of reason.[20] Reason is the *proximate* justification for natural law. The claim that God is the source of that law is a faith assertion about the *ultimate* justification of natural law that does not *necessarily* limit one's ability to know that law through reason alone. Therefore, the potential to know the general principles of the law is the same for all, believer and nonbeliever alike.[21] Aquinas's position on the knowledge of the moral law through right reason has been consistently affirmed throughout Catholic tradition.[22]

Not only do the BGT and revisionism accept these basic assertions of the natural law tradition, but they also accept similar definitions of ethical terms. The definition of positive ethical terms *(good, right, obligatory)* is that which facilitates "integral human fulfillment," "authentic personhood," or "the dignity of the human person." The definition of negative ethical terms *(bad, wrong, forbidden)* is that which frustrates "authentic personhood." Logically, if both the definitions of ethical terms and the justification of ethical and value judgments coincide, then it would seem that the norms that either frustrate or facilitate the attainment of authentic personhood should be the same as well.

However, in the normative ethical realm, these two groups of moral theologians disagree fundamentally on specific norms that facilitate or frustrate "authentic personhood." (For example, the two groups disagree fundamentally on whether the use of artificial birth control or masturbation for seminal analysis either contributes to or detracts from authentic personhood.) From this disagreement a basic question arises: What is it that fundamentally divides revisionism and the BGT, both of which are grounded in the Catholic natural law tradition? According to Timothy O'Connell, these two approaches "have entered into conflict to the point that they can be viewed accurately as alternative and competing methodologies within the natural law tradition."[23] The normative conclusions of each theory differ because their methods for deriving moral truth from natural law differ.

Method and the Sources of Moral Knowledge

On the relationship between ethical theory and method, Abraham Edel notes, "One of the greatest difficulties today is a lack of communication among the different kinds of inquiries that are going on. This produces misunderstanding as well as duplication, and the outcome sometimes is the familiar battle of schools without clarification of the way in which the issues might be resolved."[24] Edel's statement is quite apropos for the debate between revisionism and the BGT. An investigation of method in Catholic ethical theory is an attempt to clarify the fundamental differences between the two theories in order to facilitate dialogue between them. To that end, we embark on our investigation of Catholic normative method. In this text, method is defined as *establishing, investigating, and interpreting the sources of moral knowledge for justifying one's meta-ethical claims and the normative ethic one derives from those claims.* Charles Curran notes that Catholic moral theology generally accepts four sources of moral knowledge for justifying its claims to moral truth: reason, experience, scripture, and tradition.[25] *One's normative method prioritizes, interprets, and coordinates these sources into a comprehensive and comprehensible ethical theory.* Though both revisionism and the BGT are natural law theories, their respective normative methods distinguish them fundamentally. We will first describe the sources of moral knowledge and then indicate the method of each theory in light of them.

Since the Council of Trent and the development of moral theology as a distinct theological discipline, reason was frequently used as the most basic source of moral knowledge within the Catholic natural law tradition. It was this focus on reason, at least in part, that led Vatican II to call for a greater use of scripture within moral theology. However, according to the natural law tradition, faith and divine revelation do not contradict reason; they radically confirm it, albeit from a unique perspective. More recently, especially in *Gaudium et Spes* (Pastoral Constitution on the Church in the Modern World), the importance of experience has been emphasized as a source of moral knowledge.[26] Experience "recognizes more than the rational and also includes an a posteriori way of moral learning."[27] It is a truism that "experience is the greatest teacher." With regard to Christian ethics and method, this phrase is apropos. Many of the novel ethical questions that we are confronted with and attempt to resolve arise and often find unique and insightful resolution through experience. Experience provides invaluable knowledge and insight into moral truth. Moral judgments are the concrete manifestation of human experience and are the very source of ethical discourse, as we have noted above. Reason and experience are grounded in creation and the human person and provide knowledge for the ongoing discernment of moral truth.

Within the Christian tradition, however, reason and experience can be limited sources of knowledge. Human reason is tainted by the reality of sin—personal, original, and social—that can corrupt our ability to analyze moral issues accurately, honestly, and objectively. For the same reasons, experience may tempt one to determine moral truth in and through simple majority or consensus. Consequently, these sources are complemented by revelation, or God's self-communication to humanity. Revelation takes the form of scripture and tradition. Any Christian ethic that takes its identity seriously must clearly demonstrate the role and function of revelation in its ethical theory. This is especially the case in the Catholic natural law tradition, given the peripheral role of revelation, primarily scripture, throughout its history.

With regard to scripture as a source of moral knowledge, the BGT and revisionism agree on several points. First, scripture is the heart of theology, including moral theology. Second, as noted by Vatican II's *Dei Verbum* (Dogmatic Constitution on Divine Revelation), scripture must be read from a historical critical perspective.[28] The Pontifical Biblical Commission's document, *The Interpretation of the Bible in the Church,* further confirmed the legitimacy of the historical critical method as well as new methods and theories of interpretation.[29] The point of these documents is similar. One must utilize contemporary biblical exegetical tools to discern the original meaning of the text in relation to the audience and culture for which it was written and, in light of that meaning, attempt to discern its present meaning in a radically different historical-cultural context. This is no easy task. In addition, both agree that, given the promise of the Holy Spirit to guide the church, the church is the primary and authoritative teacher of scripture. As we shall see in Chapter 4, however, "the church" as authoritative teacher has very different connotations for these two schools of thought. Nor is this the only difference that separates the two groups regarding scripture.

In using scripture as a source of moral knowledge, one must remember not only that scripture must be read in its historical and cultural context, but also that there are numerous authors and books in scripture that were written over hundreds of years. As a result, there is not a single theological perspective in scripture from which moral theology can draw. Rather, the theological perspectives are as diverse as the authors and the communities for which they wrote. The theological perspective one adopts when formulating one's ethical theory will have profound implications on the shape that theory will take. Thus, scriptural scholars often refer to a "canon within a canon" that reflects a particular emphasis of biblical texts and the theologies that those texts develop. As we shall see in Chapter 3, the BGT and revisionism give priority to different scriptural texts in formulating their ethical theories.

While scripture was written in a particular time and place for a particular people, it is an ongoing narrative that is constantly being retold and relived in the lives of believers. Tradition hands on this lived narrative. The living tradition of the Catholic Church is precisely that, living, changing, and evolving. While there are certain fundamental truths such as the incarnation and Trinity that are at the heart of Christian identity, our *understanding* of these truths evolves and develops in light of history, culture, reason, knowledge, and experience. This evolution applies not only to dogmatic truths, but to Christian ethics and praxis as well. Christian ethics must evolve and develop in light of contemporary moral questions and challenges. Tradition interprets and applies scripture in ever new and appropriate ways through the working of the Holy Spirit within the church. There are two relevant senses in which tradition is used in this text. Tradition with a capital "T" is the process of handing on; tradition with a small "t" is the content handed on.[30] A fundamental difference between revisionism and the BGT is on the role, function, and authority of Tradition and tradition in either ethical theory. In respect to Tradition, the question of authority within the church and the ecclesiologies that the view of authority reflects is central. Concerning tradition, "the hermeneutic problem is to discern the difference between continuing a content that expresses divine revelation and a teaching that merely reflects the sociological and cultural circumstances of a particular time and place."[31] The role and function of Tradition and tradition in these two theories will be developed in Chapter 4.

Catholic Normative Method: Revisionism and the BGT

Both revisionism and the BGT use these sources of moral knowledge to develop their normative method. The prioritization, function, and interpretation of these sources distinguish their ethical theories fundamentally. Normative method prioritizes, interprets, and coordinates these sources into a comprehensive and comprehensible ethical theory. Investigating the normative methods that fundamentally differentiate revisionism and the BGT is the project of this work. A cursory overview of these methods lays a structure for the following chapters.

The project of revisionism reflects its historical development and consists of two investigations. The first investigation emphasizes the philosophical dimension of natural law. Much of the early work of revisionism drew upon philosophical ethics to develop what the manualists had neglected, a normative method. Both the questions addressed and the sources the early revisionists used highlight the inclusive nature of natural law accessible to all on the basis of reason and experience. Revisionism's development of the philosophical dimension of natural law attempts to justify concrete norms that prescribe or prohibit right or wrong acts.[32] This project is concerned with the objective realm of ethics and the impact of acts on human persons and reality. It is in this realm, the realm of philosophical natural law and concrete norms on right or wrong acts, that revisionism claims that there is not a specific Christian ethic.[33] Even so, the ultimate justification for this philosophical natural law relies upon revelation. The basis for our trust in experience and reason as sources of moral knowledge is that God has created the universe and that universe is good; moreover, God has created human beings in God's image and likeness. Thus, even philosophical natural law is not based purely on reason and experience alone.

The second investigation of revisionism emphasizes the theological dimension of natural law. As revisionism has evolved, it has become increasingly focused on the specificity of Christian ethics. This specificity, however, applies not to concrete norms on right or wrong acts, but to the human subject, his or her identity, motives, and perception.[34] The concrete right or wrong acts that a person chooses may be the same for all people, but the reasons for those choices are fundamentally different for Christians. The movement toward virtue ethics and spirituality in relation to Christian ethics are at the core of this development in revisionism's theological investigation of natural law. From this perspective, revelation takes precedence over reason.

The revisionist method differs depending on whether it is developing a philosophically oriented natural law ethic defining and justifying an objective, concrete norm (i.e., proportionate reason) for distinguishing right or wrong acts or a theologically oriented natural law ethic addressing the subjective identity, motives, and perceptions that Christianity provides. In the philosophical project, reason and experience take precedence over revelation, though revelation offers an implicit justification for that rational approach. In the theological project, revelation takes precedence over reason, though reason is necessary for formulating, expressing, and incorporating revelation into that project. Thus, the interrelationship between the sources of moral knowledge depends upon the natural law project being addressed. For revisionism, it would be accurate to list the four sources of moral knowledge as a hermeneutical circle whereby "all four sources relate to one another and mutually correct one another."[35] The revisionist method attempts to balance these sources, depending on the project being pursued.

The BGT could be divided into philosophical and theological dimensions as well. Philosophically, its theory is grounded in reason, though it is sometimes suspicious of experience as a source for moral knowledge.[36] Anyone who is familiar with the BGT recognizes that, while claiming to be a thoroughly rational ethical theory, it is a staunch defender of official Catholic magisterial moral teaching.[37] This institutional commitment creates a tension between its philosophical and theological dimensions.

Philosophically, while it claims to be thoroughly rational, theologically it recognizes that rationality is inherently limited and perfected through faith. Not only can faith correct reason, but it also adds normative content that is inaccessible through reason alone. While revelation is obviously the primary source of its theological dimension, its understanding and interpretation of revelation differs fundamentally from that of revisionism. Tradition, more specifically the magisterium, is the ultimate interpreter of all sources of moral knowledge. In fact, while the BGT would posit reason as the primary source of moral knowledge philosophically, theologically reason is subject to the authoritative judgments of the magisterium.[38] As such, there is a strict hierarchy of the sources of moral knowledge in the BGT based on the magisterium's authority to interpret those sources. While it is the case that scripture is the fundamental source of all theology according to the BGT and, therefore, the primary source of moral knowledge, the interpretation of scripture as well as all the other sources of moral knowledge are subject to the authoritative judgment of the magisterium. This hierarchy is Tradition (magisterium), scripture, reason, and experience. It is in this hermeneutical sense that Tradition (i.e., magisterium) is the primary source of moral knowledge in the BGT.

Our investigation into the different hermeneutic and prioritization of the sources of moral knowledge will allow us to gain some insight into what fundamentally divides these two interpretations of natural law theory. In the following chapters, we will present the two theories (Chapter 1) and investigate how reason, experience (Chapter 2), scripture (Chapter 3), and (T)tradition (Chapter 4) function in either normative ethical theory. Finally, we will briefly conclude with suggestions for future research to discover a "method of common ground" that may facilitate dialogue between revisionism and the BGT.

1
Natural Law: The Basic Goods Theory and Revisionism

Currently, Catholic moral theology is facing what can accurately be described as a schism. The schism is between two interpretations of natural law and centers on the methodologies that each theory utilizes to defend its interpretation. The genesis of this schism focused on the question of absolute norms. Revisionism, which utilizes proportionate reason and has frequently been referred to as proportionalism, is the school of thought that systematically questioned the existence of some moral absolutes in Catholic teaching whereas the BGT defended them.[1] And while the exchanges between these two groups have tended to focus on absolute norms, this is just one methodological element of ethical theory. This chapter will present the BGT and revisionism's principle of proportionate reason and explain the common criticisms that are leveled against each position. The following chapters will focus on other methodological dimensions that distinguish the two theories at the foundational level and are central to the debate on Catholic normative method.

Before investigating the methodological differences between the two interpretations of natural law theory, we should first explain those aspects upon which both the BGT and revisionism agree. First, each theory accepts natural law as an objectivist or universalist meta-ethical theory. That is, both groups recognize that there is universal moral truth and that truth can be justified through reason and revelation. Second, both the BGT and revisionism see shortcomings with the traditional Catholic natural law as it was developed in the manualist tradition and seek to revise the implicit method that the tradition used. Third, both would define *right* or *good* as that which facilitates "integral human fulfillment," "authentic personhood," "the human person adequately considered," "human flourishing," or some other variant of this concept, though the definition "authentic personhood" and the norms that facilitate or frustrate it differ in each theory. Fourth, they agree that both faith and reason are essential in the revision of Catholic moral theology, and further, that reason and revelation are not diametrically opposed but complement one another in justifying normative claims for what facilitates authentic personhood. Fifth, they recognize the importance of the four sources of moral knowledge—reason, experience, scripture, and T(t)radition—in developing a normative method, though they assign different weight to these sources and frequently have a fundamentally different hermeneutic for interpreting these sources. Finally, in reaction to the weaknesses of the manual tradition, both emphasize the need to reintegrate spirituality or ascetical theology and moral theology.

Given the agreements between the two theories, what is it that distinguishes them fundamentally? Most basically, what distinguishes these two groups is their acceptance or rejection of negative absolute material (revisionism's term) or absolute specific (the BGT's term) norms (i.e., rules that proscribe certain behavior always and everywhere) and intrinsically evil acts (i.e., actions that are always wrong). These two issues, however, need further qualification. While both would recognize that there are absolute moral norms, they differ on what types of norms are absolute. Also, while they would both agree that certain acts are intrinsically evil, it very much depends upon how the act is described and what are considered the morally significant components of the act.[2] For example, while the BGT would classify the use of artificial contraception between a married couple as an intrinsically evil act, this would not necessarily constitute such an act for revisionism. Both would agree, however, that murder is an intrinsically evil act. One can see, then, that what is at stake in much of the debate between these two groups hangs on definitions. What do we mean by intrinsically evil acts? Are there different types of norms, and what norms can be considered absolute? Before answering these specific questions in Chapter 2, we will present an overview of the two theories and common criticisms directed toward each theory from the opposing camp. We will then illustrate the fundamental normative difference between them in their resolution of a concrete moral issue.

Critique of Traditional Natural Law

The BGT, sometimes referred to as the "traditionalist" school, is both traditional and revisionist. It is traditional in the sense that it supports the magisterium in its moral pronouncements and emphasizes the hierarchy's preeminent authority to interpret and to teach the truths of salvation. In another sense, it is "revisionist" both theologically and philosophically. Theologically, the BGT heeds the call by Vatican II to revise moral theology.[3] In this renewal, according to Grisez, two things require equal attention: "the nobility of the calling of Christians and their obligation to bring forth fruit in charity for the life of the world."[4] Philosophically, it has developed a method referred to as the "New Natural Law Theory" or what we refer to as the BGT.[5] This theory is grounded in reason and defends specific absolute norms.

To better understand the BGT, it is helpful to reflect briefly upon its critique of the traditional natural law, most aptly formulated by Aquinas, with distinct nuances throughout Christian tradition, especially in the period of the manuals. According to Aquinas, natural law is a "light of reason which is in us, inasmuch as it can show us goods and direct our will, because it is the light of God's countenance—that is, a light which derives from his countenance."[6] The self-evident practical principles of natural law provide a foundation for norms for human behavior, e.g., "the good is to be done and pursued; the bad is to be avoided."[7] The main objection to Aquinas's theory of natural law voiced by D. J. O'Connor (and accepted by John Finnis) is that Aquinas fails to explain "just how the specific moral rules which we need to guide our conduct can be shown to be connected with allegedly self-evident principles."[8] At the root of this question is the insight, developed by David Hume[9] and known as the naturalistic fallacy, that it is logically invalid to derive an "ought" (a value judgment or obligation) from an "is" (a fact). The BGT accepts this position. Though Aquinas is not guilty of committing this logical fallacy according to the BGT, his natural law theory needs to be nuanced to explain why this is not the case and, further, to establish logically the connection between specific moral norms and self-evident principles.

In the view of the BGT, the later moral manualists' use of Aquinas—known as the Scholastic natural law theory—did commit the naturalistic fallacy and also had many other shortcomings that it seeks to correct. First of all, the BGT argues that to posit the given reality of human nature as the basic moral standard and then to judge acts as either moral or immoral based upon whether they conform or do not conform with that nature is logically unacceptable. Scholastic natural law "confuses the normativity of nature with the normativity of human practical reasoning";[10] it takes actual human nature and derives moral obligations from it. Second, Scholastic natural law's use of nature as its norm created a moral theology based on negativism and minimalism.[11] That is, it indicates those actions that do not conform to human nature and are, therefore, forbidden, but these negative prohibitions do not positively direct one's life toward growth and human flourishing. In such a system, the basic question is, "What must I do to avoid hell and attain heaven?" This is the minimum requirement, and the strict formulation of the law based on human nature provides those guidelines, but nothing more. Third, this theory's use of nature as the source for norms creates a static moral theology. Human nature is essential and unchanging and, therefore, the norms that conform to that nature are as timeless and unchanging as that nature itself. Finally, this theory is grounded in laws rather than persons. To counter all of these criticisms, the BGT posits goods that fulfill human persons as the foundation for its theory.[12]

The Basic Goods Theory

To fill the "gap" in Aquinas's natural law theory and correct the mistakes of the Scholastic natural law theory, Germain Grisez, John Finnis, Joseph Boyle, et al., propose the BGT.[13] This new approach is a theory of moral judgment based on the self-evident first principle of practical reason (FPPR), the first principle of morality (FPM), and the specification of that principle into modes of responsibility from which specific norms are derived. Practical reasoning underlies human action and guides it. Before indicating what ought to be done, it indicates what might be done. Both phases are essential to practical reasoning. According to Aquinas, the first principle of all practical reasoning is that "the good is to be done and pursued; the bad is to be avoided." According to Grisez, the FPPR "articulates the intrinsic, necessary relationship between human goods and appropriate actions bearing upon them."[14] This principle and its variations are self-evident and indemonstrable, though they are neither innate nor inferred from anything. With this qualification, the BGT avoids the accusation that its theory derives an "ought" from an "is": We do not know the FPPR through our interaction with the natural world or even our awareness of human nature.[15] This general principle, however, does not tell us what to do; it merely indicates what is involved in doing anything whatsoever. Consequently, there must be a way to distinguish between what is truly good and merely an apparent good. The FPPR, then, needs content. Basic goods, though very general, provide content to this principle.[16]

The basic goods are "aspects of our personhood, elements of the blueprint which tells us what human persons are capable of being, whether as individuals or joined together in community."[17] We come to an awareness of basic goods in and through our experience of a natural inclination toward them. Finnis summarizes: "By a simple act of non-inferential understanding one grasps that the object of the inclination which one experiences is an instance of a general form of good, for oneself (and others like one)."[18] There are two subdivisions that constitute eight basic goods. The first three are "nonreflexive" or "substantive" goods (human life [including health, physical integrity, safety, etc.], knowledge and aesthetic appreciation, and skilled performances of all kinds). These goods "are not defined in terms of choosing, and they provide reasons for choosing which can stand by themselves." The next four basic goods are "reflexive" (self-integration, practical reasonableness or authenticity, justice and friendship, religion or holiness) "since they are both reasons for choosing and are in part defined in terms of choosing."[19] The list of basic goods has evolved. Most recently, marriage and its fulfillment through parenthood have been added as a basic good. This basic good "is a reflexive good inasmuch as the self-giving of mutual consent is included in each of its instantiations. But unlike the other reflexive goods, the interpersonal communion of marriage also is a bodily good: unity in one flesh, which is actualized by sexual intercourse and further fulfilled by family life."[20] In whole, these eight goods indicate what human beings are capable of becoming, both as individuals and in community.

The basic goods provide content to Aquinas's FPPR, but the goods are not yet moral goods.[21] All people act for a reason, and while the basic goods provide a reason for acting, one can do moral evil in pursuing one basic good while choosing to violate, impede, or destroy another basic good. Consequently, the basic goods require a moral principle that can direct us toward morally good choices where there are many possibilities for acting. This first principle of morality (FPM) is formulated thus: "In voluntarily acting for human goods and avoiding what is opposed to them, one ought to choose and otherwise will those and only those possibilities whose willing is compatible with a will toward integral human fulfillment."[22] By "integral human fulfillment," the BGT means the situation of "the *ideal community*" whereby "the freely chosen actions shaped by moral truth would bear fruit in the fulfillment of all persons in all the basic goods."[23] As such, integral human fulfillment is not one among the basic goods or even a synthesis of them. Neither is it a reason for choosing in the same sense as the basic goods. "One cannot choose 'integral human fulfillment' as such, but one can choose in a manner consistent with loving that ideal."[24] In this sense, then, "integral human fulfillment is an ideal corresponding to total human responsibility. Like the ideal of perfect love, it is something toward which one can work but which one can never reach by human effort."[25] As such, "the guidance which the ideal of integral human fulfillment offers to choice is to avoid unnecessary limitation and so maintain openness to further goods." [26]

Though moral, the FPM is very general. Consequently, the BGT provides "intermediate principles" that function as a bridge between the FPM and specific moral norms. These principles are the eight modes of responsibility. While they do not prescribe or prohibit specific acts (e.g., adultery), they do identify modes or ways of choosing that coincide with or violate the FPM. "The modes of responsibility specify—'pin down'—the primary moral principle by excluding as immoral actions which involve willing in certain specific ways inconsistent with a will toward integral human fulfillment."[27] More specifically, "each mode of responsibility simply excludes a particular way in which a person can limit himself or herself to a quite partial and inadequate fulfillment."[28] The eight modes of responsibility are as follows: 1. "One should not be deterred by felt inertia from acting for intelligible goods"; 2. "One should not be pressed by enthusiasm or impatience to act individualistically for intelligible goods"; 3. "One should not choose to satisfy an emotional desire except as part of one's pursuit and/or attainment of an intelligible good other than the satisfaction of the desire itself"; 4. "One should not choose to act out of an emotional aversion except as part of one's avoidance of some intelligible evil other than the inner tension experienced in enduring an aversion"; 5. "One should not, in response to different feelings toward different persons, willingly proceed with a preference for anyone unless the preference is required by intelligible goods themselves"; 6. "One should not choose on the basis of emotions which bear upon empirical aspects of intelligible goods (or bads) in a way which interferes with a more perfect sharing in the good or avoidance of the bad;" 7. "One should not be moved by hostility to freely accept or choose the destruction, damaging, or impeding of any intelligible good"; and 8. "One should not be moved by a stronger desire for one instance of an intelligible good to act for it by choosing to destroy, damage, or impede some other instance of an intelligible good...."[29] Any possible choice that violates one or more modes of responsibility is, by definition, prohibited. The eighth mode is at the heart of absolute specific norms and is at the core of the debate between the BGT and revisionism.

Finally, from these modes of responsibility one can derive specific norms for behavior that characterize acts as wrong, good, obligatory, or permissible.[30] Since the focus of the debate between the BGT and revisionism is on absolute, negative norms, it is important to describe the BGT's process of formulating such norms and their impact on moral judgments. "First one considers how the voluntariness involved in a certain kind of action is related to basic human goods. Next one considers the moral determination, which the modes of responsibility indicate for this relationship. From these two premises one deduces the negative moral determination of that kind of action."[31] "Moral norms direct human acts, but they primarily bear upon choice. They bear upon the rest of life to the extent that it is shaped by the will."[32] As such, the acts that norms specify apply not so much to outward performances or even the impact of the act on *objective* reality, but rather to an intrinsic relationship between the object of choice and the willing subject who chooses the act.[33] For example, it is not the act of extramarital intercourse that defines the object of choice as adultery, but the intention to commit adultery, regardless of whether or not one in fact carries out the act.[34]

Typically, we accept the norms handed on to us by various sources (e.g., don't lie) without questioning those sources or the foundation of those norms. Sometimes, however, it becomes necessary to look at the whole rational process of formulating norms, especially when new ethical questions arise (e.g., cloning). In the case of developing an entirely new norm, one must proceed with "an accurate analysis of the act and application to it of moral principles."[35] (We will further explain the normative reasoning used in this process in Chapter 2.)

According to the BGT, specific norms are either nonabsolute or absolute. Nonabsolute norms are those norms whereby a change of circumstances or additional information can change the moral specification of an act that requires a more specific norm to govern that act.[36] Absolute norms, however, apply to acts whereby the very willingness to perform them constitutes a will that is necessarily incompatible with an openness to integral human fulfillment.[37] In its defense and justification of absolute norms, the BGT reaffirms the magisterium's teaching (albeit with a more developed ethical theory than traditional natural law arguments) that there are some acts that are intrinsically evil, i.e., they can never be justified morally. These acts include lying, adultery, and deliberate contraception, among others.

Up to this point, the BGT is grounded in reason and, therefore, defends a universal ethic. Through revelation, however, the BGT is transformed through faith and charity of the individual Christian into a specifically Christian ethic.[38] As a result, there are specifically Christian norms derived from the FPM and the modes of responsibility that are transformed through the Sermon on the Mount in Matthew's Gospel. The formula for the Christianization of the modes of responsibility, called the modes of Christian response, is the following: A mode of responsibility, specified by faith and fulfilled by charity, becomes a mode of Christian response that corresponds to one of the eight Beatitudes.[39] (We will expand on the methodological claim for how this transformation takes place in Chapter 3.)

In summary then, the BGT accepts Aquinas's FPPR. The eight basic goods specify the good to be pursued and are the basis for practical reflection and deliberation. "To identify them is to identify expanding fields of possibility which underlie all the reasons one has for choosing and carrying out one's choices."[40] The FPM requires that we have an appreciation for all the basic goods and choose only those possibilities that are directed toward integral human fulfillment, which is expressed in, but not identical to, those goods. The eight modes of responsibility serve as both primary specifications of the FPM and the foundation for the formulation of any specific norm.

Revisionism and Natural Law

While the BGT is one revised interpretation of natural law in Catholic moral theology, it is not the only interpretation. Revisionism has attempted to revise the traditional understanding of natural law in light of contemporary philosophical, theological, and scientific developments grounded in human experience. Like the BGT, it is both traditional and revisionist. This theory is traditional in that it recognizes the importance of tradition as a source of moral knowledge and the role and authority of the magisterium in interpreting and teaching the truths of salvation. However, unlike the BGT, which attempts to provide arguments justifying the magisterium's moral teachings, revisionism is sometimes critical of those teachings based on the magisterium's ethical reasoning, especially in the case of some absolute norms. As a result, revisionism questions not so much the *content* of norms that the magisterium teaches—e.g., many revisionists recognize the premoral values the magisterium is protecting in its teaching against artificial contraception—but the *classification* of those norms as absolutes. It rejects this classification of the norm precisely because it does not find the magisterium's reasoning convincing. Revisionism is revisionist both philosophically and theologically. Philosophically, revisionism formulates a norm or criterion grounded in reason and experience for determining the *objective* rightness or wrongness of acts. This criterion is called proportionate reason and designates the school of thought known as proportionalism. While revisionism, as it is used in this text, entails this school of thought, it goes beyond the determination of objectively right or wrong acts. Theologically, it is concerned with discerning the impact of Christian faith and charity on the *subjective* dimension of a person's identity, perceptions, and motives in pursuing right or wrong acts[41] as well as investigating how scripture and tradition are utilized methodologically in developing Christian ethics.

While revisionism would generally accept the BGT's account of practical reasonableness and the natural inclination toward the basic goods and integral human fulfillment, it fundamentally disagrees with the eighth mode of responsibility that to directly "destroy, damage, or impede" a basic good is always an immoral act.[42] Of course, what this denial entails requires a precise definition of "basic goods," "direct," "destroy, damage, or impede," and what revisionism calls "proportionate reason" that could justify destroying, damaging, or impeding a basic good. While proportionate reason will be defined in this chapter, the other three concepts will be addressed in Chapter 2. The clarification of these concepts is what is at the heart of the criterion of proportionate reason and revisionism's philosophical natural law project.

Before defining proportionate reason and its relationship to revisionism's philosophical project, however, we will first give a brief historical account of the genesis of this project. In 1965, a German theological student by the name of Peter Knauer wrote an article[43] that, while merely seeming to clarify a traditional Catholic principle, carried "through a revolution in principle."[44] The purpose of this article was to reexamine "the principle of double effect," not as it was understood in traditional Catholic teaching of the manuals, but as it was to be "rightly" understood,[45] as Knauer believed Thomas Aquinas had proposed it.[46]

Although it led "a marginal existence in the handbooks of moral theology,"[47] the manualists did use the principle of double effect to determine what was directly and indirectly willed in an action of conflict that involved a good and bad effect or consequence. For example, the act of self-defense might entail two effects, one good (self-preservation) and the other bad (death of the assailant). The question with which the manualists struggled was whether or not the bad effect could be morally justified. The principle of double effect attempted to answer this question. Though stated in various ways, the four criteria of the principle of double effect were formulated as follows: 1. "...the act may not be 'evil in itself' from the beginning"; 2. "...the evil effect of an act may not be what is actually wanted; this effect may therefore not be directly intended"; 3. "...the evil effect may not precede the good effect as a means. This seems to mean that the evil effect may not be the evil means in order to reach a good purpose"; and 4. "...for the allowance or causation of the evil effect, one should have a 'proportionate reason.'"[48] If the four criteria were fulfilled, then the evil associated with the act was deemed indirect, and therefore morally acceptable. In the manualist use of the principle of double effect, the direct/indirect distinction was morally decisive in determining whether or not an act with two effects was morally permissible. The late Richard McCormick, S.J., the most influential proponent of revisionism in the United States, notes that as time passed the directness of certain acts became identified with the object of the act itself (e.g., direct killings and direct sterilizations) and these acts were considered intrinsically evil. "In other words, the visible procedure began to define the intentionality, rather than the over-all intentionality defining the procedure."[49] Even in cases of conflict, one could not utilize the principle of double effect to determine whether or not such acts could be morally justified since these acts failed the first criterion, i.e., they were defined as intrinsically evil by their very object.

Knauer challenges the manualist understanding of the principle of double effect. The essence of Knauer's position is that the four conditions constituting the principle of double effect can be reduced to the requirement for a proportionate reason.[50] Whereas traditionally the principle of double effect made the direct/indirect distinction morally decisive, Knauer posited proportionate reason as the morally decisive factor.[51] Furthermore, other revisionists argued that the direct/indirect distinction itself was not entirely helpful because it could be used either in a moral sense or a descriptive sense. Only in the former sense did it have a bearing on discerning the moral nature of the act. For example, while the descriptive intent of practicing artificial birth control could be defined as preventing conception, the moral intention could be defined as practicing responsible parenthood. While the former may be morally objectionable, the latter, according to revisionism, may be morally acceptable in certain situations. Unfortunately, this distinction was not always acknowledged and led to the condemnation of certain acts based on a descriptive definition of intention.

Proportionalism and Proportionate Reason

Though the genesis of proportionalism can be linked to Knauer, its evolution has taken on many forms with various distinctions and conceptual clarifications throughout its historical development. One of the most basic distinctions requiring clarification is what proportionate reason *is* and what it is trying to *do*. Both those who defend and critique proportionalism are sometimes unclear about what they are defending or critiquing. For example, proportionalism is referred to as a "method for making moral judgments,"[52] "principle and method,"[53] "structure of moral reasoning,"[54] "teleological theory,"[55] "teleological principle," "normative method," "consequentialism," "moral theory,"[56] etc. While some of these labels share a great deal in common, others are quite distinct, and deal with different realms of ethical discourse.[57] For example, as Garth Hallett points out, there is a very important but often overlooked distinction between a "norm" (directing conduct) or "criterion" (defining right conduct) on the one hand and a "method" (defined by Webster, e.g., as "a systematic procedure, technique, or mode of inquiry") on the other. "A single valid criterion may define right and wrong, but the clues that correlate with the criterion, and the corresponding methods of discerning right and wrong, may vary widely."[58] So, whereas proportionate reason is a norm for directing one toward right acts, the method for justifying this criterion can be found in various sources including scripture, tradition, reason, and experience. Not to differentiate these realms of ethical discourse, however, results in a great deal of confusion.[59]

Although proportionalism itself has not always been clear in its initial formulation concerning what exactly was being developed (e.g., a method or norm), this is understandable. Proportionalism was attempting to revise fundamentally a moral system that, for the last 400 years, had served a very specific function and purpose in Catholic tradition, i.e., to train seminarians to hear confessions. As the discussion has progressed, however, proportionalism has become increasingly concerned with establishing a consistent and coherent use of terms and conceptual classifications. This applies most basically to the foundational concepts of the revisionist normative method, proportionalism and proportionate reason. James Walter notes an important distinction between these two terms. Proportionalism is "the general analytic structure of determining the objective moral rightness and wrongness of acts and of grounding [material] behavioral norms." Proportionate reason "is the moral principle used by proportionalists to determine concretely and objectively the rightness or wrongness of acts and the various exceptions to behavioral norms."[60] The focus of proportionalism and proportionate reason is on the rightness or wrongness of acts, not the goodness or badness of the moral agent. Since this insight has only come to light gradually in the revisionist discussion, it is not always recognized or adhered to consistently.[61]

While the discussion of revisionism has evolved as a *theological* natural law ethic, and includes an investigation into the foundation and formulation of character norms that identify the impact of Christian faith on character, identity, perception, and motive, this was not always the case. Initially, proportionalism as a philosophical natural law ethic was not concerned with *formulating* norms for behavior. Bernard Hoose echoes this point in noting that "a careful examination of the writings of proportionalists reveals that they do not in fact propose a method."[62] If proportionalism does not propose a normative method, it cannot *formulate* norms. In fact, to my knowledge, revisionism has never denied the validity of any norm *in se* taught by the magisterium and the premoral values that those norms seek to promote and protect. What revisionism does question is the classification of those norms as *moral* absolutes: "A prescriptive behavioral norm can be exceptionless only if it prescribes a value that cannot in principle come into conflict with other values."[63] The acts prescribed or prohibited by prescriptive behavioral norms deal exclusively with premoral values and premoral disvalues.

> When they emphasize the prefix 'pre' in premoral values and disvalues, proportionalists refer to the fact that these values/disvalues really do exist independently of our free will. When they emphasize the 'moral' aspect in pre*moral* values and disvalues, revisionists point to the fact that these values/disvalues are always relevant to our moral activity and therefore must always be taken into account.[64]

Since premoral values/disvalues can and do conflict, behavioral norms cannot be absolute. Revisionism provides a norm or criterion (proportionate reason) for resolving cases of conflict on the level of moral judgments when two norms conflict, e.g., the prohibition against the use of artificial birth control within the marital relationship and the need to limit one's family size in order to practice responsible parenthood. Certainly revisionism recognizes the premoral values protected by both norms. In the realm of moral judgments, however, revisionism argues that in every act premoral values and disvalues conflict. Proportionate reason is a means of resolving this conflict. It is inaccurate, then, to say that proportionalism is a method for formulating *behavioral* norms. One could say that proportionalism has formulated a single, formal[65] norm (that one must have a proportionate reason for causing premoral disvalue), but this does not constitute a normative method. As a formal norm, proportionate reason challenges the magisterial classification of absolute norms and provides a norm or criterion for resolving conflicts when behavioral norms or premoral values and disvalues conflict.

Within normative ethics itself, the distinction between the act and the norm is very important. Until one has a comprehensive understanding of what constitutes an act and the aspects of the act (e.g., consequences) that determine its rightness or wrongness, one cannot be clear as to the content and nature of the norm that prescribes or proscribes that act. Proportionate reason analyzes the aspects of an act that determine the act's rightness or wrongness. Those aspects include consequences (both short and long term, to the extent that these are foreseeable), context or situation, premoral values and disvalues, institutional obligations, relational considerations, the traditional circumstances,[66] and any other consideration that would influence an overall analysis of an act's rightness or wrongness. Having loosely defined the aspects that determine an act's rightness or wrongness, proportionate reason analyzes whether or not a contemplated act corresponds to a material norm that could be followed unequivocally, or if there is a competing norm at stake. Since all acts contain premoral values and disvalues, the material norms prescribing or prohibiting an act are nonabsolute norms. That is, if and when it is determined that there is no *excessive* conflict between the premoral values and premoral disvalues pursued in an act, the norm is to be followed. The term *excessive* indicates that the very premoral value sought in one's act is threatened by a premoral disvalue in the contemplated act, its consequences, and the other aspects that determine an act's rightness or wrongness. Proportionate reason is the formal norm for making this assessment. Given the complexity of those aspects that determine an act's rightness or wrongness, however, those norms can only be tentative or, in the words of W. D. Ross, *prima facie* norms.[67] That is, all things being equal, the norm applies. As a result, revisionism refers to material norms as "nonabsolute" rather than "absolute" norms since the very definition of an act does not entail an absolute character but is very much context dependent for its analysis and the determination of its rightness or wrongness.

Proportionate reason, then, functions as a formal norm or principle for moral judgment to resolve cases in which two or more norms conflict or there is excessive conflict between the premoral values and disvalues of a contemplated act. There are many misperceptions about the meaning of the terms *proportionate* and *reason*. *Reason* does not mean some serious reason, or even a good intention that would justify the premoral disvalue in an act. Nor does it mean "the total net good" of an act, as is the case in consequentialism. Rather, by *reason* is meant "a premoral, i.e., a conditioned and thus not an absolute, value which is at stake in the total act." It is the "*ratio* in the act…the premoral [value] the agent seeks to promote."[68] Similar to the misinterpretation of *reason, proportionate* is frequently considered a "mathematical measuring" or "weighing." As such, it is readily identified with utilitarianism or consequentialism and easily dismissed as a principle for moral judgment from a Christian perspective. This, however, is a misinterpretation of the term. "…'Proportionate' refers to a proper relation *(debita proportio)* that must exist between the premoral disvalue(s) contained in or caused by the means and the end *(ratio)* or between the end and the premoral disvalue(s) contained in the further ends (consequences) of the act taken as a whole."[69] A proportionate reason, then, is not strictly a weighing or balancing of the total net good of the consequences of an act. While consequences are important in determining whether or not a proportionate reason exists, the consequences are just one consideration along with other aspects mentioned above that both define the act and determine its rightness and wrongness.

There are certain criteria for determining whether or not a "proper relation" exists between the premoral value(s) and disvalue(s) of the means and end or the end and further ends. Investigating these criteria would take us beyond our current task.[70] Suffice it to say that even among moral theologians who consider themselves proportionalists there is a great deal of disagreement about these criteria. In fact, establishing a working set of criteria is a central component of the ongoing development of proportionate reason as a formal norm for determining right or wrong acts. What proportionalists would agree on, however, is that proportionate reason reveals a deeper epistemological perception about reality and human interaction within that reality. Moral judgments on what is a right or wrong act are often riddled with conflict and ambiguity. Proportionate reason as a principle or norm is meant to assist the agent in the decision-making process. If a contemplated act unambiguously conforms to a behavioral norm, then the norm is to be followed. According to revisionism, all of our acts involve premoral values and disvalues. At the very least, the premoral disvalue of choosing a premoral value is that it eliminates the possibility of pursuing another premoral value simultaneously. (For example, I cannot choose the premoral value of writing this book and spend quality time with our twin boys at the same time.) Consequently, proportionate reason is relevant to every moral judgment that a human being makes, even though in most cases the agent does not consciously reflect on this ambiguity, and merely follows the norm. Proportionate reason becomes explicit when the premoral disvalues that permeate all human activity are on a level that threatens the very premoral value that one is striving for in one's act. The development of criteria for determining when the premoral disvalue is counterproductive to the premoral value sought in one's action is by no means definitively established in proportionalism. Following Aquinas, prudence[71] would be the ultimate determinant for whether or not a proportionate reason exists, and the variables entailed in the exercise of prudence are infinite, thereby defying strict criteria. Nonetheless, human beings are incredibly adept at making such judgments.[72] This does not, however, absolve revisionism from the necessity of seeking to formulate criteria that will help to explain and also to facilitate this process.

In summary, then, proportionate reason functions as a norm or criterion for moral judgment in determining whether or not a nonabsolute, material norm applies in a particular situation. If it does, then the norm is to be followed. If it does not, then one may further specify the norm. (For example, Aquinas states that reason dictates that goods entrusted to another person should be returned to their owner. However, if one is keeping another's weapon and the owner wishes to use it for unjust purposes, then the norm requiring one to return another's property is further specified by the consideration of the circumstance, unless that person intends to use the property in an unjust manner.[73]) One may also apply another norm. Or, one may determine which act will produce the greatest premoral value over disvalue in this particular situation. In a sense, one could say that proportionate reason is the "trump" norm when there is a conflict between norms or excessive conflict between premoral values and disvalues in a contemplated act. Only in such cases does one resort to proportionate reason.

In her analysis of the debate between the BGT and revisionism, Jean Porter notes a fundamental difference between the first principle of morality (FPM) in each theory. For revisionism, the FPM might be stated as "always act in such a way as to bring about the greatest possible balance of premoral goods over premoral evils, given that you can do so without directly bringing about moral evil."[74] Before we address the most common critiques between the BGT and revisionism, we must first comment on Porter's formulation. Whereas the BGT's FPM is a basic principle for its entire ethical theory, philosophical and theological, as stated, revisionism's FPM, which corresponds to proportionate reason, is a norm or criterion for determining right or wrong acts. As such, it does not address the subjective dimension of revisionism's theological project that focuses on how Christian faith affects one's perception, identity, and motive. For the BGT, however, the FPM is grounded in the subjective dimension of the willing subject, regardless of the objective impact of those acts on reality. As Grisez and Boyle note, "Precisely what an individual intends in choosing to do something defines his or her action, and we call what is intended *the content of the proposal adopted by choice.*"[75] For example, it is not the *act* of murder that makes it murder, but the *intention* of the willing subject to commit murder, regardless of whether or not one in fact does so. Even the definition of objective morality differs radically between the two schools of thought. For revisionism, objective morality is defined as the impact of an act on reality, regardless of the subjective motive of the act. For the BGT, objective morality is "constituted by what people think they are doing."[76] The differences in focus of the FPM of either school highlight fundamental differences in the projects of the theories themselves.

BGT's Critique of Revisionism

There have been numerous, and oftentimes heated, exchanges between the BGT and revisionism. Certainly the stakes in the debate were raised by Pope John Paul II's publication of *Veritatis Splendor* in 1993 that condemned "proportionalism" or "teleologism" as a method of ethical reasoning.[77] Though revisionism denies that the encyclical accurately reflects its position and, therefore, is not a condemnation of it, nonetheless, that condemnation has deepened the abyss between the BGT and revisionism. As advocates of the magisterial position, albeit with an ethical theory that sometimes challenges its argumentation but rarely its moral conclusions,[78] the BGT has made it a central aspect of their own theory to discount proportionalism as a viable "rational method of moral judgment." We will focus on three criticisms that the BGT makes against proportionalism. First, the BGT claims that proportionalism requires that two incompatible conditions be met. These are "first, that a moral judgment is to be made, which means both that a choice must be made and a wrong option could be chosen; second, that the option which promises the definitely superior proportion of good to bad be knowable." According to Grisez, these two conditions cannot both be fulfilled.

> If the first condition is met and the morally wrong option could be chosen, then its morally acceptable alternative must be known. Otherwise, one could not choose wrongly, for one chooses wrongly only when one knows which option one ought to choose and chooses a different option....But when the first condition is met, the second cannot be. The option which promises the definitely superior proportion of good to bad cannot be known by a person who chooses an alternative which promises less. If the superior option were known as superior, its inferior alternative simply could not be chosen.[79]

According to this critique, then, proportionalism fails as a "method of moral judgment." Rather than guiding choices, it logically prevents them. According to this first critique, then, "proportionalism is not false but absurd, literally incoherent."[80]

The second critique of proportionalism focuses on the incommensurability of basic goods. The basic goods are incommensurable in the way that proportionalism requires to carry out its project.[81] Grisez writes:

> If a [proportionalist] admits that justice and theoretical truth, or any other two goods, are fundamental and incommensurable, then the [proportionalist] also admits that "greatest net good" is meaningless whenever one must choose between promoting and protecting or impeding and damaging these goods in some participations. For if these goods really are incommensurable, one might as well try to sum up the quantity of the size of this page, the quantity of the number nineteen, and the quantity of the mass of the moons as to try to calculate with such incommensurable goods.[82]

All of the basic goods must be respected equally, as demonstrated by the seventh and eighth modes of responsibility. One can never directly attack one basic good to obtain another because to do so would entail commensuration and, since the basic goods are incommensurable, this is impossible. So, for example, justice and truth are fundamentally different values. As such, there is no possible common denominator for a comparison between the two that would allow proportionalists to make a rational judgment of the greater premoral value if the two come into conflict.

If, however, proportionalism could establish a hierarchy of goods, then it would have grounds for claiming commensurability (i.e., based on that hierarchy one could compare basic goods and determine that this basic good is more important than another basic good in a particular situation). The consideration of whether or not there is an objective hierarchy of goods is the basis of the BGT's third critique of revisionism. According to the BGT, there is a sense in which there is an objective hierarchy of values, for example, "moral good can be ranked higher than nonmoral, intelligible good higher than merely sensible good, basic good than instrumental, divine and human than animal, heavenly than earthly."[83] None of these comparisons, however, is of the type that proportionalism requires. Why not? Because proportionalism "was to have been a rational method of moral judgment, and a rational method should determine what is right and wrong before one chooses."[84] What is at the heart of this critique, as Grisez discusses elsewhere, is the equivocation of the term *decide,* which can mean both to "judge" and to "choose." "When 'decide' refers to judgment, it is a matter of detecting what is right and wrong; when it refers to choice, it is a matter of doing what is right and wrong."[85] Grisez admits that a hierarchy is adopted and commensuration does take place in choice. However, "proportionalism requires comparison of goods in a moral judgment antecedent to choice; when commensuration occurs in choice itself, the time for moral judgment is past."[86] By positing commensuration in choice, then, proportionalism shows its true face, a theory of rationalization.

That is, first one chooses the act one will do and then finds a proportionate reason to justify that choice.

Revisionism's Critique of the BGT

Revisionism responds to the BGT's "no choice," incommensurability, and hierarchy of goods critiques and, in so doing, posits its own critique of the BGT. First, Garth Hallett points out that the BGT's "claim of necessity" (i.e., if one knows which option offers the greatest value, one simply could not choose any other option) conflates the desirable and the desired. That is, "define the good, subjectively, as 'anything a person can in any way desire,'" and, "whatever a person finds attractive…is ipso facto good. Whatever a person finds more attractive is ipso facto better. Perceived value and felt attraction cannot conflict. However, in the objective sense of *value*…perceived value and felt attraction can indeed conflict, and often do."[87] Consequently, even though a person might know the "definitely superior" choice that offers the greater good, he can still choose a lesser value. To deny such a possibility is to deny the reality of sin. The BGT may respond that one can indeed choose the lesser value in this case, but that choice would not be rational.[88] This, however, posits a very narrow anthropology whereby in moral judgments the human is a purely rational being. A central tenet of revisionism is that sinful reality, both personal sin and the sin of the world, not only affects our ability to choose rationally, but also imposes conflict on such choices. In light of such realities, both the agent's ability to perceive objective values and to choose those values is limited. Reason, whether it is in judging premoral values or disvalues or choosing among them, is frequently limited by human finitude and the constraints of reality.

The BGT's second critique focuses on the incommensurability of the basic goods. Revisionism would concur with the BGT that the basic goods, as basic, are incommensurable. On more than one occasion, Richard McCormick has endorsed the

BGT's notion of basic goods.[89] However, these basic goods are more like Platonic ideas[90] than goods that facilitate actual moral judgments of right or wrong acts. As basic, the goods are incommensurable, each fundamentally equal in relation to the other. The realm of moral judgments, however, takes place not in the abstract, within the world of ideas, but in the concrete reality of human existence. In this realm, context, premoral values and disvalues, relationships, norms at stake, consequences, etc., provide a common denominator by which basic goods can be compared, prioritized, and chosen in relation to one another.[91] Such commensuration, however, does not require a set hierarchy of goods, since the goods at stake will vary in different situations and contexts. What commensuration does require is a norm or principle for comparing and prioritizing the basic goods or aspects of those goods when two or more of them conflict. Proportionate reason is the norm for commensuration. Many revisionists accept Louis Janssens' personalist criterion of the human person adequately considered and the eight dimensions of that criterion that facilitate the moral agent in determining whether or not a proportionate reason exists.[92] While commensuration of goods is not a precise science, and indeed is very difficult at times, this difficulty does not render proportionate reason meaningless, irrational, or a principle of justification. What commensuration and proportionate reason do require is that we recognize the following: 1. there are a variety of ways to arrive at a judgment of proportionality; and 2. the prudent person is the best measure of these judgments.[93]

There are three responses to the BGT's third claim that proportionalism fails because it establishes a hierarchy of goods and commensuration in choice rather than moral judgment. First, Richard McCormick notes that the BGT fails to recognize that this argument "bites back." McCormick explains his rejoinder in an exchange with Grisez on nuclear deterrence and nuclear war.

For instance, if the 'proportionalist' must choose before judgment, how is this any different from the 'nonproportionalist' who argues legitimate national self-defense against an aggressor? Does such a person not have to weigh political freedom against the loss of human life in defending it and *decide* that it is reasonable to suffer this evil for that good? If values are incommensurable for the 'proportionalist,' how are they any less so for the person applying the fourth condition of the double effect (proportionate reason)? …Grisez answers as follows: 'They may not do to an enemy's population (even as a side effect) what they would not have the other nation's leaders do to them and their people. In such cases, proportionality reduces to the golden rule.'

But that is not an adequate answer. The question—which requires a rational answer if Grisez's critiques against 'proportionalists' as arbitrary deciders are to carry any weight—is: *Why* would they not want it done to themselves? Why would a war become unduly burdensome? Is it not because the overall evils do not stand in a proportionate relationship to the values to be protected or achieved? Does that not demand the very weighing and balancing Grisez says is rationally impossible?…To say that proportion is a matter of…prudence and sometimes imprecise is not to say that it is irrational or arbitrary.[94]

Second, whereas Grisez claims that proportionalism fails because it locates commensuration in choice, Finnis words this critique somewhat differently. The type of comparison that proportionate reason requires, according to Finnis, is "a rational judgment made prior to moral judgment and choice, and concerning the intelligible goods in the options available for choice." Finnis shifts the locus of commensuration from Grisez's moral judgment to a rational judgment. As a purely rational judgment, detached from context, revisionism itself admits that the basic goods are incommensurable. Revisionism, however, does not have to prove commensurability in *this realm* of practical reasoning because it accepts that the basic goods are incommensurable here. Neither does it have to prove commensuration in the BGT's FPM. For it is not the case that "the [proportionalist] claims to derive a moral norm from commensuration and not vice versa."[95] The exact opposite is the case. After considering norms and determining that *in this situation* two or more norms conflict or the premoral values and disvalues of a contemplated act conflict excessively, one resorts to a proportionate reason in order to resolve such conflicts. The context of an ethical issue provides the common denominator to commensurate premoral values and disvalues that, in reality, conflict.[96] It is somewhat ironic that Finnis posits commensurability in "states of affairs considered in abstraction from their origins, context, and consequences,"[97] but not in the concrete realm of moral judgment. Thus, it is *not* the case, as Grisez asserts, that revisionism is a theory of "rationalization." Proportionate reason and, hence, commensuration exist in the realm of moral judgment. The application of proportionate reason in moral judgment is contingent upon the context that provides the grounds for comparison or common denominator between the norms or premoral values and disvalues at stake. This reliance upon context for commensuration does not mean that revisionism is guilty of the naturalistic fallacy ("no 'ought' from 'is'").[98] Certainly the descriptive and the evaluative are in relation to one another. Even the BGT recognizes that context will determine whether or not a norm applies in a particular situation.[99]

The third response to the BGT's hierarchy of values and commensuration critique denies that this critique is even an issue. The commensurability that proportionalism requires, and that Grisez recognizes, would be fulfilled if one could posit commensurability in the realm of moral judgment. That is, moral *judgment* determines what is right or wrong, and one *chooses* in light of that judgment. We can detect a misunderstanding in Grisez's statement that we addressed briefly above concerning what proportionalism *is* and what it is trying to *do*. The BGT is positing proportionalism as a method of moral judgment. However, as we noted in comparison between the FPM of the two theories, revisionism's FPM is a criterion or norm for determining right or wrong acts when two accepted norms conflict (e.g., in the case of self-defense there are two conflicting norms: the norm calling for self-preservation and the norm forbidding one to kill). It is *not* the case, as Grisez asserts, that revisionism is a theory of "rationalization" whereby "first one makes a choice and then finds a reason for it."[100] Rather, it is precisely the norms at stake, the premoral values and disvalues of acts that those norms prescribe or prohibit and the context that necessitate recourse to proportionate reason as a "trump" norm to resolve those conflicts.

In light of revisionism's rejoinder to the BGT's critique, its own critique of the BGT becomes clear. First, in the abstract, it agrees that the basic goods are incommensurable. In the context of a moral judgment, however, basic goods do come into conflict in light of the norms at stake and the premoral values and disvalues prescribed or prohibited by those norms. The means for resolving those conflicts is proportionate reason. Second, by having recourse to the fourth criterion of the principle of double effect (proportionate reason), the BGT utilizes commensuration between goods and values in a similar way that it criticizes revisionism for using it. As Grisez notes, "One can say that the reason for accepting bad side effects is 'proportionate' if their acceptance does not violate any of the modes of responsibility."[101] The difference between the two theories is *not* in the function of commensuration (both rely on a comparison of [premoral] values and disvalues) but in the nature of the basic goods (moral or premoral) and the modes of responsibility, especially the eighth mode, that does not allow one to choose to destroy, damage, or impede a basic good. The BGT, then, is inconsistent in applying its critique on the incommensurability of the basic goods to revisionism when it depends upon commensuration as well to justify the moral judgment that this act is right while only accepting the disvalue of an act as a foreseen but unwanted side effect.

Revisionism, however, agrees with the BGT on several points. First, it accepts the first principle of practical reason

(FPPR). Second, it accepts the incommensurability of basic goods in the abstract. Third, it accepts the norms taught by the magisterium. Where it disagrees with the BGT is on the nature of these norms, absolute vis-à-vis nonabsolute. While the BGT's FPM pertains primarily to the subjective dimension of the willing subject who chooses an act, revisionism's FPM pertains to the objective rightness or wrongness of an act. In making a moral judgment on the rightness or wrongness of an act, revisionism posits proportionate reason as a norm for resolving conflicting premoral values and disvalues prescribed or prohibited by norms. An example will help to clarify the fundamental difference between these two perspectives.

An Illustrative Case: Lying to an Assailant

Grisez poses a case entitled, "Lying to enemies is incompatible with loving them." From the outset, we must make clear that since the BGT does not distinguish between objective and subjective morality in the same sense as does revisionism, the terminology relating to this case is ambiguous. Consequently, we will use the BGT's terminology (lying) and revisionism's terminology (falsehood) when presenting their respective positions. What is not ambiguous are the fundamentally different conclusions that each theory reaches in resolving the case. The specific question is whether or not it is permissible to lie to an enemy in order to protect a person from harm. A typical scenario is that a German citizen in Nazi Germany is harboring a Jew in her house. An SS soldier comes to the door and inquires whether or not there are any Jews in the house. Even if the German is reasonably certain that the SS soldier will kill the Jew, she cannot lie to him. The BGT's assessment of this case is the following:

> Since the truth is to be spoken with one's neighbor, a person must not lie even to enemies, for enemies too are neighbors.

Of course, silence is not lying, and enemies need not be provided with the truth of which they can be expected to make bad use. But even someone certain he or she was speaking with a person intent on committing murder would not be acting as love requires if, judging that person to be beyond repentance, he or she resorted to lying in an effort to save the potential victim's life. Rather, treating as neighbors both the potential victim and the enemy would require not giving the information and explaining why: "I will not answer your question and help you do wrong; instead, for your soul's sake, I ask you to repent of your wicked intent." Such an answer might or might not succeed, but it is a work of hope, while lying is an act of desperation.[102]

The reason for the assessment of this scenario and the moral judgment that is reached is grounded in the basic goods of self-integration and authenticity. Lying and other deceptions "divide the inner and outer selves of those who engage in them, contrary to their own self-integration and authenticity, while impeding or attacking the real community that truthful communication would foster, even when deception seems necessary. Therefore lying and other deception in communication are always wrong."[103] The fact that an innocent life will be sacrificed to integration and authenticity, in this case, is regrettable. However, this result cannot justify a lie, since to do so would be directly to attack or impede a basic good, self-integration and authenticity. It is interesting to note that the BGT defends its position on the basis of community. While the BGT would justify killing in self-defense, "using deadly force in defense does not impede community as lying does." This would seem to fly in the face of Grisez's own assessment on the immorality of capital punishment that violates human dignity and the sanctity of life, especially if this is considered in light of its impact on the community.[104] Does not allowing the murder of a human being have even more negative repercussions on a community than the presumably just execution of a guilty criminal by the state?[105] Revisionism has a different response to this scenario.

Revisionism could respond to this scenario in at least two ways. The first response, relying upon Grisez's description of the basic goods at stake in lying, does not, curiously enough, require commensuration for its resolution.[106] Grisez defines self-integration as "harmony among all the parts of a person which can be engaged in freely chosen action," and practical reasonableness or authenticity as "harmony among moral reflection, free choices, and their execution."[107] Regrettably telling a falsehood to protect a human life when no other option is available to protect that life would surely facilitate these two basic goods. Moreover, one could conceivably describe the act as saving a life, with the side effect of telling a falsehood, since knowledge or truth are not explicit considerations in formulating the absolute norm that prohibits lying for the BGT in this case. "One cannot lie," Grisez notes, "without choosing the self-alienation which, opposed as it is to self-integration and authenticity, *is sufficient* to make lying wrong."[108] This response raises an important point: How we define the act, its consequences, values, disvalues, side effects, etc., will have profound implications on the moral analysis of that act. Clearly, the BGT and revisionism endorse different criteria for determining what is or is not morally significant in their act-descriptions. This topic will be addressed in detail in the next chapter.

The second response requires commensurability based on a description of the norm forbidding the premoral disvalue of telling a falsehood grounded in the basic good of "knowledge of various forms of truth" (which could include a consideration of authenticity and self-integration as well). A norm prohibits telling a falsehood because it violates the good of knowledge. The competing goods in this scenario would be life (i.e., protecting life), justice, and friendship. Revisionism would posit these goods as premoral values and the attack upon them as premoral disvalues. In this case, there is an excessive conflict between the premoral good of knowledge and the premoral goods of life, justice, and friendship, since all cannot be realized in this situation. The context provides the common denominator. For example, it is reasonably certain that anything short of a falsehood would result in the death of a human being. The state is an unjust aggressor. The SS soldier has no right to the knowledge based on his use of that knowledge. The consequences will be the death of a person. Telling a truth will violate one's relational commitments to the German Jew. The community will be damaged by the ongoing tyranny of a government that executes innocent people on the basis of ethnic categories. In light of these contextual considerations, proportionate reason would justify telling a falsehood (a premoral disvalue) to protect a human life (a premoral value). It seems that any reasonable person could reach this conclusion, even though there is not a strict set of criteria for commensuration. This is not to say that the BGT is unreasonable. What it does say is that its perception of basic goods on the level of practical reasoning is distinct from revisionism's perception of basic goods on the level of moral reasoning and how they function in concrete moral judgments.

As this example illustrates, the BGT and revisionism themselves are incommensurable. The incommensurability resides partly in the definition and understanding of basic goods and whether or not these goods are commensurable in concrete moral judgments and partly in the definition of the components that determines an act's goodness or badness (in the case of the BGT) or rightness or wrongness (in the case of revisionism's proportionate reason). More basically, however, the normative ethical methods of each theory differ fundamentally on the sources of moral knowledge and the hermeneutic and interrelationship between those sources in developing their method. We will take up an investigation of these in the following chapters.

2
Reason, Experience, and Method

Throughout much of the history of Catholic moral theology, reason was seen as the most basic source of moral knowledge within the Catholic natural law tradition. It was this focus on reason, at least in part, which led Vatican II to call for a greater use of scripture within moral theology.[1] However, according to the natural law tradition, faith and divine revelation do not contradict reason; they radically confirm it, albeit from a unique perspective. More recently, the importance of experience has been emphasized as a source of moral knowledge.[2] Experience provides invaluable knowledge and insight into moral truth. Reason and experience are grounded in creation and the human person and provide knowledge for the ongoing discernment of moral truth.

Within the Christian tradition, however, reason and experience can be limited sources of knowledge. Human capabilities to reason are tainted by the reality of sin—personal, original, and social—that can corrupt our ability to reason accurately, honestly, and objectively about moral issues. Experience, as well, may tempt one to discern moral truth in and through a simple majority or consensus.

While reason and experience are essential to both ethical theories, within the BGT there is a curious tension in its use of these sources depending on whether it is viewed as a philosophical or theological ethic. Its philosophical ethic is grounded in reason.[3]

Theologically, reason becomes subordinate in that, "when the results of philosophical ethics are used by moral theology, they must be evaluated and transformed by incorporation in the more adequate view of reality provided by the truth of faith."[4] Experience is a questionable source of moral knowledge, according to the BGT, especially if it leads to dissent from the "constant and very firm moral teaching of the Church."[5] (Of course, this statement presumes definitions of what constitutes "constant" and "very firm," which will be treated in Chapter 4.) Nonetheless, both reason and experience as sources of moral knowledge are subject to the authoritative interpretation and judgment of the magisterium.[6]

With its focus on material norms and right or wrong acts, reason and experience are foundational sources of moral knowledge for revisionism's philosophical project. This is fully consistent with the Catholic tradition's acceptance of Aquinas's assertion that views the natural law as the "participation of the eternal law in the rational creature."[7] Still, it is only because of its theological foundations, which posit the goodness of creation as a source of moral knowledge and human beings as created in the image and likeness of God, that discerning moral truth is possible. To fully grasp the philosophical methodological division between the BGT and revisionism, in this chapter we will investigate reason and experience and their role and function in each ethical theory.

Reason and Method

Norbert Rigali, S.J., noted some years ago that "many a contemporary moralist is in the unenviable position of lacking a scientific grasp of the epistemological foundations of his own field."[8] Epistemology is central to ethics since to claim that something is good presumes a way of knowing what is good. Epistemology and our understanding of the good are in an ongoing dialogue. As our claims about what is good change, so too does our epistemology. Similarly, as our epistemology evolves and develops, so too does our understanding of the good. While moral theology has come a long way in developing an epistemological foundation, epistemology is, and remains, at the heart of differences between, and among, ethical theories. Both the BGT and revisionism agree on foundational components of a natural law ethical theory. First, they accept Aquinas's classic definition of natural law. According to Aquinas, natural law is a "light of reason which is in us, inasmuch as it can show us goods and direct our will, because it is the light of God's countenance—that is, a light which derives from his countenance."[9] The self-evident practical principles of natural law provide a foundation for norms for human behavior, e.g., "the good is to be done and pursued; the bad is to be avoided."[10]

Second, the BGT and revisionism[11] accept the theory of basic goods. The basic goods are "aspects of our personhood, elements of the blueprint which tells us what human persons are capable of being, whether as individuals or joined together in community."[12] We come to an awareness of basic goods in and through our experience of a natural inclination toward them. John Finnis summarizes: "By a simple act of non-inferential understanding one grasps that the object of the inclination which one experiences is an instance of a general form of good, for oneself (and others like one)."[13]

While both theories would accept the rational inclination toward the basic goods and authentic personhood as the foundation of ethics, different understandings of the goods due to divergent epistemologies radically differentiate the normative claims of each ethical theory. In the following section, we will investigate the impact of each theory's epistemology in relation to the basic goods, worldview, and anthropology.

Epistemology and Philosophical Ethics: Naturalistic Fallacy or Ethics Detached from Persons and Nature?

How do we know the basic goods? Following Thomas Aquinas, both schools of thought accept that humans have a "natural inclination" toward the basic goods.[14] Furthermore, both reject the naturalistic fallacy—the attempt to define an ethical term with a natural or metaphysical term, or to identify an ethical judgment with a factual judgment; no "ought" from "is."[15] Consequently, both posit the basic goods as self-evident, rational grounds for choice. Considerations of persons and nature and their impact on the knowledge and particular exemplifications of the basic goods differ for each theory, however.

In the BGT, these considerations seem to pose serious epistemological concerns regarding its claim to absolute norms, the causal or logical relationship between the will and object of choice, and act-descriptions. First, the BGT argues that there are absolute, universal norms derived from the basic goods, the first principle of morality (FPM)[16] and its specifications in the modes of responsibility. However, how can one ground such norms in basic goods that are "not definite objectives," that "transcend any particular state of affairs which can instantiate them,"[17] and "are open ended"[18] with "endless ways of serving and sharing in them"?[19] From some revisionist's perspectives, such basic goods appear to be generic goods, infinitely detached from concrete reality and human persons, and belong in the realm of Platonic ideas.[20] In his review of Finnis' *Natural Law and Natural Rights,* John Langan highlights this tension: "One thing that is not clear in Finnis' approach is the connection between a basic [good] in its general form and its particular exemplifications."[21] While basic goods that belong to, and remain within, the realm of ideas are not necessarily problematic for ethical theory, they become problematic if one claims them as a foundation for absolute norms.

Second, to avoid the naturalistic fallacy, the BGT denies the causal relationship posited by traditional moralists between an act and a willing subject that provides objective grounds for morally assessing the agent's will.[22] In the BGT, then, one can bring about an effect in the realm of physical causality and not will it directly. That is, "people intend only what they choose as a means or seek as an ends." In its discussion of direct intention and the nonabsolute norm of killing for the sake of self-defense, "one must take care not to import any notion of behavioral or physical directness, such as that expressed by *straightaway,* or any other notion of temporal immediacy or spatial proximity."[23] So, in the case of a woman shooting a would-be rapist in the head, "her end is to avoid being raped; her means is to prevent the would-be rapist from carrying out the behavior which would constitute rape."[24] The causal link between the death of the would-be rapist and the woman's avoiding being raped is merely an unintended side effect of the act of self-defense; it is neither willed as an end nor chosen as a means. If there is no causal relationship between act and intention, however, what is the relationship? Jean Porter posits that it must be a logical relationship. That is, "if the agent's aim in acting can be logically described with reference to the good that she seeks, without mentioning the harm that she brings about, her act is morally licit; otherwise not." In which case, "the agent's intention could be described in terms of whatever could be said to be the agent's purpose or motive in acting."[25] While it is clear that the BGT would reject this analysis of its theory (since that would put it in the subjectivist camp, which it adamantly opposes), it is difficult to see why this conclusion would not follow from its reasoning. In the case of a nonabsolute norm, where the distinction between direct intention and indirect intention could justify certain unintended side effects, the denial of a causal relationship between the basic goods, nature, and persons claims too little. Depending on how one describes the intention of the willing subject, as long as the unintended side effect is not directly intended, killing or any other act that is not prohibited by an absolute norm is morally permissible.

While the BGT's position on the relationship, or lack thereof, between physical causality and the morality of an act chosen by a willing subject also would be accepted by revisionism as well in certain instances (e.g., self-defense), the BGT is selective in the types of acts in relation to the willing subject that are open to such noncausal descriptions. In the case of the absolute norm prohibiting artificial birth control, for example, the relationship between basic goods, nature, and persons claims both too much and too little. The BGT posits a *necessary* relationship between contraception and a will that directly attacks the basic good of life. As Grisez and Boyle write, "Contraceptors *necessarily* foresee that a baby might come to be, they want that foreseen baby not to come to be, and they choose to do something in order to make it less likely that he or she will be."[26] Even if a person intends a further good by practicing contraception, his or her will, by definition, is contralife. "Therefore, considered as a moral act, each and every contraceptive act necessarily is contralife."[27] However, why is it that, in the case of self-defense, there is no necessary relationship between the act of wounding or killing an assailant and intention to defend oneself, while in artificial birth control, the BGT posits a necessary relationship between contraception and a contralife will? Is it logically necessary that the primary intention of a married couple that uses artificial birth control, regardless of further intentions, be contralife? To justify this claim, Grisez focuses on the indivisibility of the act in the case of self-defense, and two or more distinct acts in the case of contraception. In the case of self-defense against a rapist, there is a single indivisible act including both the directly intended object (self-protection) and the unintended side effect (injury or death of the assailant).[28] In the case of contraception, however, there are two or more distinct acts. One act is contraception. "In and of itself, a contraceptive act is nothing but contralife. For, being distinct from any sexual act that occasions it, a contraceptive act cannot be considered part of that sexual act, even if the outward behaviors involved in the two acts are closely associated."[29] According to Grisez, it is necessary (if one will excuse the pun) that contraception be conceived as a single, indivisible act. If it could be seen as part of a sexual act, then it is feasible that artificial contraception could be morally justified according to the principle of double effect, much like self-defense is morally justified. "However, the principle of double effect is not correctly used to justify what is done in one act by the good features of another, distinct act."[30] The other act or series of acts are sexual expression, responsible parenthood, etc. The first act is a direct attack on a basic good, regardless of any acts that follow after it.

Grisez offers two arguments for why contraception and a sexual act are two distinct acts. First, one can practice contraception independently of a sexual act. For example, a man might be sterilized and yet not find a person with whom to engage in sexual intercourse. Second, a couple considering fornication has two choices to make: whether or not to fornicate and/or contracept. The contraceptive act does not entail the sexual act in either scenario.[31] Edward Vacek, S.J., challenges Grisez's claim that contraception is a single act and not part of a sexual act. In the first case, the person sterilized intends the sterilization to be part of one's sex life; otherwise, the sterilization would be self-mutilation. Since intention is decisive for Grisez in determining what an agent does, however, the intention to sterilize is necessarily part of one's sexual life. Applying the logic of the second scenario to the case of sex between a married couple, one might be forced to conclude that sex in this case is not a marital act. This is so because some people have intercourse outside of the marital relationship and others make two distinct choices in choosing to be married and choosing to make love.[32] So it does not necessarily follow that contraception is a single act distinct from a sexual act.

There seems to be no rational justification, then, for Grisez's claim that there is a necessary relationship between a contralife will and contraception *unless* one posits a causal relationship between the choosing will and the physical structure of the act. Since Grisez has denied the moral significance of this causal relationship, however, it seems that one is left with Porter's logical relationship. As Porter and Vacek both correctly point out, however, there is no necessary logical relationship between a contraceptive act and a contralife will.[33] Just as the intention in self-defense is open to a variety of descriptions depending on the willing subject, unless there is a causal relationship between the willing subject and contraception, the same could rationally be claimed with regard to this absolute norm. In the case of an absolute specific norm, then, the BGT claims too much of the relationship between the basic goods, persons, and nature whereby there is a necessary link between the act absolutely prohibited and the willing subject. However, it also claims too little of this relationship by denying any causal relationship between an act and a willing subject.

While revisionism agrees that one cannot logically derive an "ought" from an "is," it attempts to give a more thorough and consistent consideration of nature and the human person in relation to the basic goods. As Josef Fuchs, S.J., notes, while the facts of nature do not declare morality, "they remain relevant for arriving at valid ethical statements about concrete, worldly conduct."[34] In addition, the full complexity of a concrete act, both its factual and evaluative components, must be taken into consideration in determining the human significance of the act as a whole.[35] Whereas morality resides in the willing subject for the BGT, sometimes in relation to nature and persons and sometimes detached from them, revisionism posits a dynamic relationship between persons, nature, and right or wrong acts. As a result, the BGT's claim that one can participate in the basic goods in a variety of ways[36] is granted its true significance within revisionism. There is not an a priori causal or logical relationship between the willing subject and the particular exemplifications of the basic goods for revisionism. Their particular exemplification takes place in the historical and concrete reality of human persons.

The particular exemplifications of the basic goods in both theories are directly related to worldview and anthropology.

Historical Consciousness

A worldview is both how one perceives the world in which knowing takes place and the epistemology one develops in light of that perception. Worldview has profound implications for the nature of moral knowledge, basic goods, norms, and human acts.

The two worldviews of Catholic tradition are classicism and historical consciousness.[37] Classicism asserts that natural law is static, necessary, fixed, and universal. Hence, the normative content of natural law is timeless, universal, and immutable, and the acts condemned by that law are always so condemned. Historical consciousness, grounded in existentialism, fundamentally challenges this view of reality. According to an historically conscious worldview, reality is dynamic, evolving, changing, and particular. While both the BGT and revisionism reject the classicism of the manuals, they differ in their interpretation of "historicism" as it shapes moral knowledge.

Grisez states that "an adequate moral theory must look toward possible human fulfillment, and its vision of this must be as dynamic as humankind itself."[38] However, elsewhere he notes that "historicity does not exclude but demands insight into the unity of each basic good of human persons, a real unity over time and place which cannot be limited without arbitrariness to the contingent conditions of the here-and-now which delimit one's present point of view."[39] Any authentic development in moral knowledge from a historically conscious perspective, then, is dependent upon maintaining the unity of each basic good. And while norms can change and develop on the basis of an "unfolding understanding of the human good," in the case where "aspects of the human goods…are already understood,"[40] no such development is possible.

There are some important questions for the BGT regarding the authentic development of aspects of basic goods in light of historicism. First, how are the basic goods divided into "aspects"? Second, what constitutes an aspect of a basic good that is open to further understanding and an aspect of a basic good that is not? Third, what are the criteria for determining when and if the dynamic dimension of humankind requires a further understanding of an aspect of a basic good versus an aspect of a basic good that is definitive? Why is it that an aspect of the basic good of justice and its unfolding that allowed slavery but now forbids it is an authentic development,[41] whereas other norms grounded in aspects of the basic goods do not allow for such development? Also, if the development of one aspect of a basic good and the norm derived from it have repercussions on another basic good, how can one determine whether or not that norm violates another aspect of a basic good unless there is some basis for comparison between the basic goods and/or their aspects? This question becomes all the more perplexing, given that the basic goods are incommensurable, according to the BGT.[42] It would seem that integral human fulfillment, which "moderates the interplay" of reasons for acting that the basic goods provide,[43] requires criteria for establishing the precise "interplay" of the basic goods. While the modes of responsibility provide these criteria, there seems to be a more fundamental criterion when it comes to specific absolute norms. As we shall see, from the theological perspective of the BGT and ethics (as compared to purely philosophical ethics) the magisterium is the definitive judge of whether or not an aspect of a basic good, and the norm deduced from it via the modes of responsibility, can be revised. This criterion is grounded in authority, however, and not necessarily in reason.

Revisionism has made historical consciousness a foundational point of its ethical theory. It is, in a sense, the *sine qua non* of revisionism. Historical consciousness applies to all sources of moral knowledge—reason, experience, scripture, and tradition—and the interaction between these sources. There are important implications of historical consciousness for the meaning, knowledge, and particular exemplifications of the basic goods. While recognizing the universal appeal of basic goods, historical consciousness relates those goods to particular human experience and persons. As universals, the basic goods may be incommensurable. As the instantiation of goods that provide a rational basis for choice by a human being, the basic goods are subject to a hierarchy depending on the particularity of the human situation. While identifying the epistemological criteria for establishing such a hierarchy has been an admitted weakness of revisionism, from a historically conscious perspective such a hierarchy is necessarily contingent on human experience and the development of human understanding and knowledge. As an ethical theory grounded in historical consciousness, revisionism, by definition, is somewhat contingent. The project of establishing epistemological criteria for a hierarchy of concrete, historical goods or values is ongoing. Not only are the basic goods both universal and particular in an historically conscious worldview, but, so too, in anthropology.

Anthropology

Both the BGT and revisionism posit the universal and particular, or essential and changing, in anthropology and its relationship to the basic goods. Grisez summarizes this relationship for the BGT.

> In acting for a good, one gradually comes to perceive its possibilities more and more fully. Thus, human nature and natural-law morality are both stable and changing....Stable, in that the givenness and fundamental unalterability of natural inclinations account for the unalterability of the principles of natural law; but also changing, in that the dynamism of the inclinations, their openness to continuing and expanding fulfillment, accounts for the openness of natural law to authentic development.[44]

Elsewhere, Grisez claims, "Although essential human nature does not change, in the course of human history new possibilities do open up and humankind acquires powers to act in new, more complex ways."[45] If the basic goods are "aspects of persons, not realities apart from persons,"[46] what is the relationship between essential human nature, inclinations, and basic goods? The BGT posits this relationship in terms of a basic inclination toward the human goods as an intrinsic and unchanging aspect of human nature. For example, the basic inclination toward life would not change to a basic inclination toward death. Human nature and the inclination toward basic goods are constant. However, since there are infinite ways of sharing and serving in the basic goods, the inclinations toward those goods are changing as well. According to this perception of the basic goods, they serve as the foundation "of a permanently valid normative ethics, whose norms are grounded, not in a demand to conform to human nature, but in the vocation to unfold the possibilities of human persons."[47] The BGT criticizes the new morality for using historicity to show that human nature could change. However, since it "cannot show that there are human persons for whom life, knowledge, friendship, and so forth are not basic goods," this theory need not be taken seriously.[48]

Far from asserting that there are human persons for whom the basic goods are not essential, revisionism would fully affirm this point. What it would debate is the meaning of the basic goods in relation to the human person. Revisionism also recognizes the essential and changing in anthropology. *Gaudium et Spes* laid the foundation for a personalist objective criterion of morality in its section on marriage and the family. It asserts, "The moral aspect of any procedure…must be determined by objective standards…based on the nature of the human person and his acts."[49] The official commentary on this document noted that this general principle applies to all human activity.[50]

Out of these documents, revisionist Louis Janssens developed his objective criterion, "the human person adequately considered," based on eight dimensions or aspects.[51] He specifically refers to these as "dimensions" rather than "definitions" to highlight the fact that our knowledge of them is both essential and changing. It is essential to the extent that these eight dimensions constitute the essential nature of the human person. It is historical and changing to the extent that the fulfillment of the human person adequately considered evolves and changes in light of the sources of moral knowledge.

Janssens applies these dimensions of the personalist criterion to dispositions and actions. A morally good disposition is

determined by our inner attitude that must be "genuinely prepared
to place our activity as much as possible at the service of the pro-
motion of the human person" as described in these dimensions.[52]
Right or wrong actions, "as active commerce with *worldly* realities,"[53] are marked by a twofold ambiguity, temporality and spatiality. Temporality recognizes our limited ability to perform
concurrent actions. We must choose in light of various options
available. Spatiality recognizes the impact of our actions on material realities or the objective world in which we instantiate both
values and disvalues. For example, a therapeutic amputation may
be required to save a person's life (premoral value), and yet violates the integrity of the corporeal subject (premoral disvalue). A
basic question for ethics is, What is the rational basis for that
choice?[54] According to revisionism, proportionate reason is the
basis for resolving conflicts between premoral values and disvalues as particular exemplifications of basic goods or aspects of
basic goods. This principle is dependent upon the commensurability of the basic goods in the concrete and historical reality of
moral judgment, a claim that the BGT denies. As basic, the goods
are incommensurable, each fundamentally equal in relation to the
other. The realm of moral judgments, however, takes place not in
the abstract, within the world of ideas, but in the concrete reality
of human existence. In this realm, context provides a common
denominator by which basic goods can be compared, prioritized,
and chosen in relation to one another.[55]

The implications of Janssens' personalist criterion and the
ambiguity of human activity in relation to the basic goods are the
following: While recognizing that our disposition or will must be
open to all the goods, spatiality and temporality not only limit our
ability to realize those goods in action but, in some cases, even
posit those goods against one another. In such cases, proportionate reason is the principle that allows for resolution when the
instantiation of different aspects of a basic good or two or more
basic goods clash in the concrete world.

Objective and Subjective Morality

What is at the heart of the anthropological division between the BGT and revisionism and its implications for basic goods and, ultimately, absolute norms? While a full response to this question is impossible here, a fundamental difference between the two theories that sheds light on it is their respective perceptions of objective and subjective morality. According to the BGT, "moral acts are *objectively* constituted by what people think they are doing. *Subjective* morality is in the possibility of a person's confusion and/or error about the moral goodness or badness of his or her act, and in the possibility that a person's freedom to choose is impeded or blocked."[56] In neither the objective nor subjective sense of morality does the BGT view morality in terms of the impact of the act on reality. So for example, a person who *intends* murder *is* a murderer, regardless of whether or not he actually commits the act of murder.[57] Morality resides in the willing subject and is tantamount to voluntarism. Revisionism defines objective and subjective morality quite differently. Motive, which pertains to subjective morality, is the *further purpose* one intends in one's actions. To actually do what one intends pertains to objective morality. The doing of the action is dependent on contingent factors. However, as Vacek notes, a consideration of the actual deed and the contingent factors are "essential to the complete analysis of the objective morality of a deed."[58] Revisionism's primary concern in normative ethics is with defining those characteristics that determine an action's objective rightness and wrongness, not the subjective goodness or badness of the moral agent, motive, disposition, or character.

What we can deduce from the difference in objective and subjective morality and its impact on anthropology is that, whereas the BGT defines human nature, inclination, and the basic goods intrinsically in relation to the willing subject (objectively and subjectively), revisionism does so intrinsically (subjectively) and extrinsically (objectively). Since morality resides within the willing subject for the BGT, and since the basic goods are the grounds for moral judgment and rational choice, and further, since the basic goods are incommensurable, there can be no *real* conflict between the basic goods and their instantiation in moral judgments. Since morality considers both the willing subject and the objective impact of one's actions on the external world that is affected by contingent factors (e.g., Janssens' spatiality and temporality), for revisionism there are *real* conflicts between the basic goods and their instantiation in moral judgment. The objective/subjective distinction also has implications for normative method and norms. To this we now turn.

Normative Method

A central distinction between the BGT and revisionism revolves around the question of whether or not there are absolute, universal norms. At the heart of this distinction is each theory's normative method for the foundation and formulation of norms. Before embarking on a normative methodological comparison between the two schools of thought, some preliminary remarks are in order. First, Garth Hallett's warning that one must distinguish between a norm or principle and a method or procedure in ethical discourse is apropos for this discussion.[59] Neither the BGT nor revisionism has always made this distinction. While the BGT has developed a rational normative method for grounding and justifying absolute specific norms, revisionism has proposed a mixed teleological normative principle for discerning right or wrong acts when premoral values and disvalues conflict. As a result, exchanges both within and between camps may be somewhat confusing. Second, as we saw above, each theory has fundamental differences on what constitutes objective and subjective morality and, consequently, on the nature and meaning of the norms that guide these two realms. Whereas revisionism formulates norms that pertain to the objective moral realm, the subjective moral realm, and the two combined, the BGT formulates norms that pertain strictly to the objective (subjective for revisionism) realm and the willing subject.

This basic difference in perception of objective and subjective morality has profound implications for the project of normative method and somewhat limits a comparison between the two theories on this methodological dimension. Revisionism recognizes C. D. Broad's bifurcation of normative ethics into deontology and teleology for determining the rightness or wrongness of acts as they are prescribed or proscribed by material norms. Following Aristotle, Aquinas, and Kant, the BGT has viewed these terms within the wider spectrum of the moral goodness and badness of acts; that is, an act is judged morally good or bad in relation to the willing subject. In a word, the normative methodologies of both theories are somewhat incommensurable. Nonetheless, I will compare them on the basis of Broad's bifurcation of normative ethics into deontology and teleology and attempt to draw some reasonable conclusions.

One of the major points of debate within ethical discourse is the meaning of the terms *deontology* and *teleology*. The terms themselves were initially compared and contrasted as two broad approaches to ethical theory in Broad's *Five Types of Ethical Theory*. Broad's bifurcation was both meta-ethical and normative ethical.[60] On the meta-ethical level, Broad was exploring both the ontological and epistemological framework for classifying all types of ethical theories. This framework is concerned with how one defines the terms *right* and *good* (i.e., *a nonmoral, consequential attribute*), the justification for those definitions, and the relationship between the two. On the normative ethical level, Broad focused on normative method and how one defines those characteristics of an act that determine its rightness or wrongness. As he writes in *Five Types of Ethical Theory:*

> Deontological theories hold that there are ethical propositions of the form: "Such and such a kind of action would always be right (or wrong) in such and such circumstances,

no matter what its consequences might be."...Teleological
theories hold that the rightness or wrongness of an action is
always determined by its tendency to produce certain consequences which are intrinsically good or bad.[61]

In light of these two understandings of deontology and teleology, we can attempt to pinpoint fundamental differences
between the BGT and revisionism. According to the proponents
of the BGT, their theory "seeks to combine the strengths and
avoid the weaknesses of teleology and deontology." It is teleological, then, in the sense that "morality is indeed grounded in human
goods—the goods of real people living in the world of experience." It is deontological to the extent that "each person's dignity
is protected by absolute *moral* requirements, and it is never right
to treat anyone as a mere means."[62] We have seen that revisionism
endorses the basic goods as the foundation of ethics. Furthermore, the first dimension of Janssens' personalist criterion encap-
sulates Kant's categorical imperative (i.e., "Never treat a person
as a mere means").[63] The BGT's use of deontology and teleology
in this sense, however, is on the meta-ethical level.

When the BGT moves from explaining its foundation of
ethics to claiming absolute specific norms, it shifts from meta-
ethics to normative ethics. With regard to normative ethics and
absolute norms, their method is unequivocally deontological *on
certain ethical issues.* These issues primarily include truth, sexual
ethical issues, and questions surrounding the beginning and end
of life. The BGT's deontological normative method is clear on
two counts. First, it claims that the basic goods are incommensurable. A necessary requirement for any teleological normative
ethic is that premoral values or disvalues (i.e., basic goods or
aspects of those goods) are commensurable. Second, there are
certain absolute or "exceptionless moral norms"[64] forbidding specific acts that can never be chosen, regardless of consequences,
because choosing such acts necessarily violates a basic good. In
other words, no good consequence or any other circumstance can

justify choosing certain actions that directly attack, impede, or destroy a basic good (e.g., lying to an assailant to protect an innocent human being[65]).

Revisionism's proportionate reason, on the other hand, *as a mixed teleological normative principle,* assesses all the significant components of the act including, but not limited to, its consequences, to determine an act's objective rightness or wrongness. Such an assessment is made in light of the human person adequately considered. As such, *material* norms (i.e., norms prescribing or prohibiting right or wrong acts) are premoral, nonabsolute norms. That is, these norms indicate that an action *tends* to be right or wrong, but they are not moral absolutes.

Revisionism espouses a mixed or moderate deontological or teleological normative method. In the case where a contemplated act coincides with the norm, all things being equal, the norm applies (deontology). However, revisionism also recognizes the ambiguity of reality when it comes to applying the norm. This ambiguity can take at least two forms. In one case, the contemplated act includes significant right-making or wrong-making components, including consequences (teleology), which would distinguish it from the act prescribed or prohibited by the norm. In this case, proportionate reason would determine whether or not the norm should be followed or if the contemplated act is a legitimate exception to the norm. In another case, a contemplated action fulfills one norm but violates another norm. In the case of a legitimate conflict of norms (e.g., the case of self-defense), proportionate reason is used to resolve such conflicts. Since the BGT locates morality in the willing subject, the ambiguity of reality and its impact on the willing subject does not pose the same conflict between basic goods and their aspects as it does for revisionism.

It is important to note the locus of the normative ethical debate between the BGT and revisionism. While both schools agree on many ethical issues, the most inflammatory issues that have caused heated debates are primarily in the areas of sexual ethics, and questions revolving around the end and beginning of life. While the BGT is defending the magisterium's teaching on these issues (while employing a developed and nuanced normative ethical method), revisionism has challenged the reasonableness of those teachings. While normative method has been a predominant focus of the exchanges between the BGT and revisionism, the definition and understanding of norms that are proposed by each ethical theory is key to the disagreements as well.

Norms

The BGT and revisionism disagree fundamentally on the definition of norms and the acts that those norms prescribe or prohibit. Fundamental to that disagreement is the question of whether or not the ordinary universal magisterium has infallibly taught any specific natural law norms. Of course, the answer to this question depends on several considerations, one of which I will take up here, namely, What constitutes a specific norm? As revisionism has developed its ethical theory, it has incorporated an important distinction from philosophical ethical discourse, namely, the difference between the ethical terms *right* and *good*. Whereas right and wrong refer to actions and their objective impact on reality, morally good and bad pertain to motive, character, disposition, agent, etc., and refer to the subjective dimension of the human agent.[66] Morally good and bad are also used when they evaluate the combined act and motive. The three groups of norms that reflect act, character, and these two combined are material, formal, and synthetic respectively. Material norms are nonabsolute, objective norms such as "don't kill" or "don't tell a falsehood." In general, these norms describe acts physically in terms of premoral values and disvalues; that is, the impact of these acts on human relationships and reality tends to be either positive or negative. Formal norms are those such as "be just," "be loving," "be chaste." These norms pertain to the subjective dimension of the moral agent, his or her character, disposition, motive, etc. While formal norms are moral absolutes, they are contentless in that they do not indicate the material action that should be done or avoided. While we could never justify being unjust, unloving, or unchaste, formal norms do not tell us specifically what is the just, loving, or chaste action in a particular situation. Synthetic norms are absolute moral norms that combine the objective and subjective dimensions into a single moral norm. "Do not murder" refers to a bad moral act and is condemned absolutely by definition. The term *murder* includes the act prohibited by a material norm (killing), the motive prohibited by a formal norm (malevolence), and a circumstance (innocent, e.g., not someone who is attacking another person) that could qualify the norm as an absolute synthetic norm. According to revisionism, only formal and synthetic norms are absolute, and thus could be the subject of infallible magisterial teaching on specific natural law norms.

The BGT recognizes the distinction between material and formal (more accurately, synthetic) norms but rejects this as a helpful distinction. Instead, it proposes a third type of norm referred to as a "specific" moral norm. According to this norm, "the description of the act goes beyond mere behavior, yet does not go so far as to build in the moral determinant."[67] An example Grisez poses is "getting rid of unwanted children by killing them." In this norm, the act described "is morally neutral in itself."[68] The moral qualification comes by analyzing this act in light of the eighth mode of responsibility. "The absolute norm follows from the fact that killing of this sort includes in itself a will incompatible with integral human fulfillment."[69] Similarly, the norm forbidding contraception is an absolute norm because it violates the seventh and eighth modes of responsibility by directly choosing to impede new human life; contraception is contralife.[70]

What is to be said of the BGT and revisionism's definition of norms and the existence of absolutes? First of all, revisionism would question whether or not the act described by the BGT is a morally neutral act. At the very least, one would have to admit that, as stated, this act describes a premoral disvalue bordering on a moral disvalue. (That is, for revisionism, one could posit it as a virtually exceptionless norm because it seems inconceivable that there would ever be a proportionate reason to justify such an act. However, a scene from the film *The Mission,* where the Indians are condemned for a similar practice, would be an interesting scenario to investigate. Resolution of this case would depend on how one defines *unwanted.*) Second, both the BGT and revisionism agree that there are absolute norms, though they disagree on the nature and content of those norms. For revisionism, absolutes are limited to formal and synthetic norms, not to material norms. For the BGT, absolutes are limited to specific moral norms qualified morally by their violation of the modes of responsibility. Third, the BGT and revisionism disagree on the categorization of certain norms. For example, while revisionism may categorize the norm prohibiting artificial contraception as a material norm and, therefore, as a nonabsolute premoral norm, the BGT would categorize it as an absolute specific (i.e., moral) norm. Fourth, both realize that the particulars of a situation can require "further specification" of a nonabsolute norm or the application of a different norm.[71] The morally significant circumstances of a situation can determine whether another norm applies or that norm must be further specified in light of an act's re-description in order to guide one's choice. In addition, the re-description of the act entails a re-description of the will choosing the act. While the BGT and revisionism agree on several aspects of norms, a major point of contention between the two theories arises regarding absolute norms and descriptions of the act and will.

Acts

According to the BGT, some specific norms are absolute and, therefore, do not allow for a further specification of the norm or a re-description of the act or will choosing the act. Contraception, understood accurately in terms of the intention involved, is always contralife.[72] An accurate analysis of the act of in vitro fertilization "is inevitably to will the baby's initial status as a product."[73] Certainly, when the act and corresponding will or motives are *defined in this way,* the act and the norm forbidding it are absolute. This description of the act is tantamount to the revisionist synthetic norm that, as we have seen, is a moral absolute. The significant question in the cases cited (and, in fact, the case of all absolute norms) is whether or not, *by definition,* certain motives *necessarily* correspond, logically or causally, to certain acts. Could one practice contraception with a will directed immediately toward responsible parenthood? Or could one utilize the procedure of IVF with a will directed immediately toward love and respect for human life? Knowing couples who have utilized this technique without cryopreservation, the risk of fetal reduction, or the destruction of embryos, and with a joyful and loving anticipation of the new life to be brought into existence and made a member of their family, one would be hard pressed to describe their primary motive or even part of that motive as willing their child as a product. Revisionism would certainly recognize that indeed it is possible to use contraception (or natural family planning) with a contralife motive or to initially will the baby that results from IVF as a product. However, it would reject the BGT's claim that there is an intrinsic link between certain acts and the will that chooses them that precludes a re-description of the will in relation to the act. In other words, revisionism would reject the necessary connection that the BGT posits between certain acts and the orientation of the will that chooses those acts. Whereas the manualists were frequently criticized for their physicalist tendencies (i.e., defining the morality of the act on the basis of its physical characteristics), revisionism could accuse the BGT of *physicalist voluntarism* whereby there is an ontological correlation between the will and act that neither reason nor experience can challenge. It is the role and function of experience in each ethical theory that attempts to either establish and justify the claim of an intrinsic moral link between certain acts and the will that chooses those acts, or disqualifies it as a necessary link.

Experience and Method

Experience is a key source for moral knowledge throughout Christian tradition. Norms and principles both arise out of human experience and judge that human experience. Certainly the Christian scriptures, both Old and New Testaments, are accounts of human interactions with, and experiences of, God. It is these experiences that are at the very heart of Christian identity. Vatican II supports the role and function of experience in formulating moral truth.[74] The ongoing ethical question is the extent to which experience can either refine or transform the meaning and content of norms or is susceptible to evaluation and judgment by those norms.

The BGT, Experience, and Method

For the BGT, there is a strict division between what one might label authentic and inauthentic experience in ethical method and its relevance for the knowledge and formulation of moral truth. Authentic experience consists of two types. The first type is an awareness of natural dispositions, "which is a sort of experience,"[75] whereby people come to know the self-evident first principles of morality. Our experience of inclinations toward these principles and the basic goods that they represent are a source for moral truth. A second type of experience is required to comprehend possible choices, which represents an "awareness of human abilities and the opportunities for their exercise offered by various situations."[76] Grisez connects this type of experience to the knowledge and understanding of specific norms. "While the truth of specific moral norms flows from that of moral principles…the understanding of those norms presupposes the experience required to understand the actions shaped by them."[77] Accordingly, then, authentic experience *in general* does not facilitate shaping a specific norm; it merely provides the understanding of the actions prescribed or proscribed by the specific norm. There are some cases in which experience can transform our

FOUR SISTERS INNS

(800) 234-1425 • www.foursisters.com

Healdsburg • Glen Ellen • Sonoma • Yountville • Napa
San Francisco • Santa Cruz • Monterey Peninsula
Santa Monica • Claremont • Newport Beach • Dana Point

understanding of an aspect of a basic good and the norms derived from the specifications of the first principle of morality (FPM). As we shall see below, however, the criteria for what does and does not constitute such transformative experience are not entirely clear in the BGT.

According to the BGT, there are two types of inauthentic experience in moral theory. The first refers to "awareness of people's actual standards and behavior (which can be described by polls and surveys, and studied by historians and social scientists)."[78] The second refers to "the process of trial and error by which people learn how to achieve concrete goals (and so acquire technical knowledge)." Neither of these types of experience, however, "provides dependable moral norms."[79] Why do they not do so? To illuminate the first type of inauthentic experience, the BGT distinguishes between social and cultural norms and specific moral norms based on moral truths. Although social and cultural norms may be accepted on the basis of experience by a particular culture and society, this experience does not demonstrate that they are morally sound. These norms must be judged by moral truth. As Grisez notes, social and cultural norms "are not standards of morality superior to the principles and norms human beings naturally know—principles and norms reaffirmed and further specified by God's revelation, which is handed on by the Church's belief and teaching."[80]

The second type of inauthentic experience is trial and error or a certain pragmatism that, while indicating through experience what might work, does not indicate what is good. Here, the BGT directly targets revisionism.

> The desirability of having satisfying experiences and avoiding suffering is taken for granted, while the prospect of a certain measure of satisfaction or misery is taken to be a proportionate reason for making exceptions to any moral norm as circumstances may require...for example, someone might discover whether adultery is morally acceptable by trying it.[81]

While Grisez acknowledges that "not all proportionalists hold so simple a theory of value,"[82] more to the point is the BGT's assertion regarding inauthentic experience in relation to foundational moral principles and specific moral norms. How do we know that adultery is intrinsically wrong, as indeed revisionism would admit? Is it because God says so? Both revisionism and the BGT would reject a divine command theory. Is it because the magisterium teaches that it is wrong? Hopefully, both revisionism and the BGT would reject a magisterial command theory as well. We know that adultery is wrong because human experience has demonstrated that performing such an act damages one's relationship with one's self, one's own spouse and family, the spouse and family of another, the social or community fabric, and ultimately with God. In a word, it is experience, not necessarily ours but that of those in the past, that is at the root of specific moral norms. This is an important insight that C. D. Broad highlighted in his work.[83] Epistemologically, deontology is grounded in experience and empirical observations that certain consequences follow from certain acts which make an act wrong in and of itself, regardless of *further* consequences.[84] Adultery is wrong not only or even primarily because God says it is wrong, but because of the damage it does to relationships. Lying is wrong because it violates the truth of speech that is presupposed for well-functioning relationships. Murder is wrong because it violates the basic dignity of another human being. Even within the Catholic tradition, one could cite numerous examples of norms, once accepted and even taught as moral doctrine, that have been revised on the basis of human experience.[85] The BGT, however, limits experience to knowing the basic goods and the norms that are deduced from the FPM and its specifications. "Neither the experience of people in former times, such as those in which slavery was accepted, nor the experience of people today is self-validating. Both must be judged by moral truth, *which cannot be learned from such experience.*"[86] A fundamental question for the BGT, then, is what constitutes this "moral truth" which is the source of specific norms and somehow independent from human experience? Let us look at one example of a norm that has evolved in the Catholic Christian tradition that both the BGT and revisionism investigate, but posit different roles to experience in their analyses of its evolution.

The BGT recognizes "legitimate development in Christian moral thought." For example, "the development of moral doctrine with respect to slavery was from condoning it to forbidding it."[87] How does such development come about? According to Grisez, this occurs "because of the unfolding understanding of the human good."[88] What causes this unfolding to take place? Instead of answering this question, Grisez attacks the "supposed development radical dissenting theologians proposed" on the basis of greater and lesser evil.[89] With regard to certain acts (e.g., adultery), such a change in moral doctrine could not occur "because the received prohibitions are based on aspects of the human goods that are already understood."[90] However, this response raises further questions. What constitutes those aspects of the basic goods that are already understood as opposed to those that are not entirely understood and are, therefore, open to development? Why is it that the aspects of the human good of justice that involve liberty in the case of slavery are open to refinement, with a corresponding revision of the norms deduced from the specifications of the FPM, while the human good of marriage and the prohibition of specific types of reproductive technologies are not? To resolve questions of philosophical ethics, the BGT has recourse to theological principles. According to Grisez, "A sound method in moral theology will not allow the moral experiences and judgments of some of the contemporary faithful to override the constant and very firm moral teaching of the Church."[91] (However, given the history of the Church's teaching on slavery prior to Leo XIII, it seems that this teaching was indeed "constant" and "very firm." It was, at least in part, the magisterium's misinterpretation of experience that allowed it to maintain its teaching in favor of slavery in the face of overwhelming experiences and rational reflections on those experiences that contradicted that teaching.)

Revisionism, Experience, and Method

Revisionism seems to give a much more credible account of how the development of moral norms takes place in light of human experience. Within revisionism, experience does not merely confirm our perception of the basic goods; it can transform those perceptions and the norms that are founded on the basic goods. John Noonan highlights experience as a source for moral knowledge in his study on the development of moral doctrine. Experience in light of human nature and the gospel allows us to judge certain actions as right or wrong. With regard to slavery, "it was the experience of unfreedom, in the gospel's light, that made the contrary shine clear."[92] Only in 1890 did Pope Leo XIII denounce the institution of slavery. This declaration of the pope reversing the norm permitting slavery came only after 200 years of experience—serious resistance, arguments, violence, political activity, and revolutions—against slavery as an institution.

Revisionism recognizes experience as a central and fundamental component of moral truth.[93] Like the BGT, it faces the challenge of discerning what is authentic experience that may transform the understanding of basic goods, principles, and the norms that follow from them, as opposed to inauthentic experience that must be judged by those principles and norms. There are certain broad categories of experience that have led to a fundamental questioning and proposed refinement of natural law norms within revisionism. We will briefly investigate four of these categories.

First, liberation theology evolved out of the experiences of the poor and oppressed in Latin America and has attempted to refine the notion of justice in light of that oppressive experience by confronting unjust social structures that institutionalize oppression.[94] These experiences have served as a hermeneutical key, not only for refining the notion of justice, but also for reading scripture and interpreting Christian tradition in light of those experiences. While not every component of the experience of the poor represents a valid basis for refining the basic concept of justice (e.g., the unjustified use of violence to bring about structural change), there are certain components of it that fundamentally alter our understanding of basic goods and the principles and norms that reflect that understanding. For example, while one can maintain the universality and incommensurability of basic goods in the abstract, divorced from human experience, in the case of the lived experiences of the poor and oppressed, the call for justice and the fulfillment of basic human needs such as food, shelter, education, medical care, etc., supercede all other basic goods. Unless and until the basic human needs to sustain life are met, the other basic goods are subordinate.

Liberation theology in Latin America gave rise not only to other liberation theologies of experience sparked by socioeconomic oppression, but also to theologies responding to gender oppression. Feminist theology is a direct offshoot of liberation theology and takes as its point of departure the experiences of women and their oppression throughout history.[95] These experiences both challenge perceptions of basic goods, principles, and norms and attempt to refine them in light of those experiences. As Lisa Sowle Cahill notes, "Feminist ethics begins with the particular, with practice, with experience, with the situation—but out of the particular (not over against it) feminists recognize what furthers or damages 'full humanity' for women and men."[96] It is the experience of women, past, present, and future, that challenges not only the perception of basic goods but also the very definition of authentic personhood. Concretely, the norm forbidding the ordination of women to the priesthood reaffirmed by Pope John Paul II[97] would be a specific norm that warrants serious reconsideration in light of these reflections.

A third type of experience recognized by Vatican II as a necessary component of reflection for morality is cultural experience. While it is oftentimes the case that the church must be countercultural, i.e., it must confront clear violations of moral truth that are deemed normative within a culture (e.g., individualism in the United States), at other times culture can be a source of discerning and communicating moral truth. In other words, cultural experience can sometimes produce insights into moral truth and facilitate the communication of a moral truth within a culture or from one culture to another. This is especially the case where a unique cultural context requires specific norms to address specific problems, as in the case of the United States Bishops' pastoral letters on the economy and nuclear war.[98] While these pastorals certainly relied upon traditional principles of justice and fairness to formulate norms that are culturally specific, this process was diachronic, i.e., the very perceptions of justice and fairness were transformed in light of the specific historical and cultural experiences to which they responded.

Finally, scientific experience, knowledge, and developments are posing new questions that require new answers. While some of these answers require a new application of principles and formulation of norms, they also challenge the very perception of basic goods themselves. For instance, the successful mapping of the human genome will have profound implications for our formulation of norms in light of the basic goods of life, knowledge, and skilled performance. New norms will have to be formulated to determine what is and is not an ethical use of medical technology to restore or maintain health. Will it be right to use genetic engineering to eliminate Alzheimer's disease, given that we do not know the full implications of "genetic tampering" on other genes? The ethical issues that such scientific knowledge will raise (e.g., an insurance company's access to genetic records) will require new norms and even a refinement of moral principles, with implications for the unfolding understanding of the basic goods. Experience and the moral knowledge it provides are at the heart of such developments.

All four of these categories of experience themselves require criteria for determining what is or is not authentic experience that can further human knowledge and understanding of the basic goods and the principles and norms derived from them. Do certain experiences require an adjustment of the specific norm, its further specification, or even its total reversal, as in the case of slavery? The answer to this question will depend on how one defines the other sources of moral knowledge, especially with regard to revelation, and the interaction between these various sources. The BGT recognizes the possible unfolding understanding of a basic good based on experience that would allow for the complete reversal of a specific moral norm, and it is very clear on the primary criterion for justifying such a development. The magisterium is the only authority that can judge in this area.[99] The rational criteria for this judgment, however, are not always clearly established by the BGT. Thus, no matter how rational the arguments grounded in experience to reverse the norm prohibiting the ordination of women to the priesthood, for example, the BGT would unequivocally conform to magisterial teaching on this issue.[100] Revisionism, on the other hand, while recognizing, respecting, and appreciating the role of the magisterium to judge on these matters, does not posit it as the ultimate determinant of moral truth regardless of the arguments proposed. History justifies such caution.

Jean Porter has critiqued both the BGT and revisionism on the basis that neither theory *defines* the basic goods with sufficient content.[101] This critique, however, is more pertinent to the BGT since it maintains the existence of absolute specific norms deduced from these undefined basic goods, the FPM, and modes of responsibility. For revisionism, the basic goods are knowable and take on meaning in and through human experience. The material norms that guide behavior, and the basic goods that are at the foundation of these norms, are contextually dependent. And, since the basic goods are commensurable given their foundation in human persons and in reality, not only are acts and the material norms governing those acts subject to development from an historically conscious perspective, but the very anthropology on which "human fulfillment" is dependent can evolve as well, with repercussions for understanding the basic goods.

To conclude our section on experience, the importance of experience in its various manifestations is summarized beautifully in *Gaudium et Spes:*

Thanks to the experience of past ages, the progress of the sciences, and the treasures hidden in the various forms of human culture, the nature of man *[sic]* himself is more clearly revealed and new roads to truth are opened. These benefits profit the Church, too. For, from the beginning of her history, she has learned to express the message of Christ with the help of the ideas and terminology of various peoples, and has tried to clarify it with the wisdom of philosophers, too.

Her purpose has been to adapt the gospel to the grasp of all as well as to the needs of the learned, insofar as such was appropriate. Indeed, this accommodated preaching of the revealed Word ought to remain the law of all evangelization. For thus each nation develops the ability to express Christ's message in its own way. At the same time a living exchange is fostered between the Church and the diverse cultures of people.

To promote such an exchange, the Church requires special help, particularly in our day, when things are changing very rapidly and the ways of thinking are exceedingly various. She must rely on those who live in the world, are versed in different institutions and specialities, and grasp their innermost significance in the eyes of both believers and unbelievers. With the help of the Holy Spirit, it is the task of the entire People of God, especially pastors and theologians, to hear, distinguish and interpret the many voices of our age, and to judge them in the light of the divine Word. In this way, revealed truth can always be more deeply penetrated, better understood, and set forth to greater advantage.[102]

Conclusion

Reason and experience divide the BGT and revisionism fundamentally on the methodological level. While the BGT attributes the ultimate authority to interpret and explain reason and experience and their relevance in discerning moral truth to the magisterium, revisionism attributes a certain autonomy to these sources of moral knowledge, regardless of whether or not the magisterium recognizes or acknowledges their contributions to the discernment process. Though the BGT's deference to magisterial authority 0 be commendable from a certain ecclesiological perspective, such deference may be at the expense of moral truth from an ethical perspective. Past errors in Catholic moral doctrine on issues such as slavery, usury, and religious freedom support a revisionist interpretation of the role and function of reason and experience in ethical method. Such errors warrant caution in positing absolute specific norms in light of conflicting arguments derived from reason and human experience.

While reason and experience are central to both the BGT and revisionism, it is largely the role and function of revelation—scripture and tradition—in either ethical theory where the heart of acrimony lies. The next two chapters will investigate these sources of moral knowledge.[103]

3
Scripture and Method

Scripture is "the soul of sacred theology," *Dei Verbum* asserts.[1] Consequently, any Christian ethic that claims to take the adjective seriously must demonstrate how scripture functions in its ethical theory. Given that the two predominant Roman Catholic ethical methods belong to the natural law tradition, the role and function of scripture in either method requires serious investigation, especially given the use of scripture in moral theology since the Council of Trent. Has either of these ethical theories moved beyond eisegesis to exegesis? That is, have they broken free from the manuals' tendency to use scripture merely as a source of proof-texts and affirmation of ethical assertions that were deduced largely from reason? In formulating ethical assertions, do they truly take into consideration revelation and its expression through scripture, as this is articulated through the work of biblical scholars under the guidance of the magisterium? What is the role and function of scripture in each ethical theory? The answers to these questions will reflect the extent to which Catholic ethical theory has taken seriously the call to renew moral theology through the incorporation of scripture and will, in so doing, shed light on the use of scripture in both ethical theories. Before investigating the role and function of scripture in either theory, however, we must briefly address the question of whether or not there is a specifically Christian ethic? The answer to this question will lay the foundation for an exploration of how revelation functions in these two theories.

Epistemology and Theological Ethics:
Is There a Specifically Christian Ethic?

In the last chapter, we investigated the relative epistemologies of each ethical theory from a philosophical perspective. In this chapter, we will do so from a theological perspective. As noted in the Introduction, there is a dialogue in Christian ethics between Christian ethical method and philosophical ethical method. This is especially the case in the epistemological realm. First of all, a basic question of the faith ethics and autonomy ethics schools is whether or not faith provides a knowledge of norms that is inaccessible to, or goes beyond, what reason can provide. As McCormick notes, the question of a specifically Christian ethic is primarily epistemological.[2] This question is fundamental to the Catholic natural law tradition given its claim of accessibility to moral truth through reason. If faith contributes no new knowledge, and Christian and non-Christian alike can arrive at the same moral truth, what, if anything, does Christian faith add to natural law ethics? On the other hand, if faith does add new knowledge to natural law ethics, in what sense is natural law accessible to right reason alone? In the former case, Christian natural law ethics would be universal without particularity; in the latter case, it would be particular without universality. As one would imagine, the BGT and revisionism have two very different responses to the question of the relationship between faith and reason and how this relationship pertains to moral knowledge. The question is not *if* faith adds anything to moral knowledge, but rather *how,* and on *what level of ethical discourse* it relates to moral knowledge.

The BGT maintains that faith transforms the human's ability to know.[3] In so doing, it provides specifically Christian norms[4] that are deduced from revelation and Christian charity. These norms do not contradict but rather fulfill those norms deduced from natural law purely through reason.[5] Since the BGT claims a specific knowledge for Christians that produces specific Christian norms, it is important to notice the epistemological flow of this specifically Christian knowledge. "The commitment of faith is the fundamental option of Christian life" for the BGT.[6] In light of this fundamental option, one's knowledge is transformed through grace, which in turn transforms one's perception of reality and the available options of choice for a person of faith. "There are specifically Christian norms because there are specifically Christian acts."[7] Here, the epistemological flow of knowledge is from the willing subject and moral judgments to specific norms. The faith of the believer is, in a sense, projected onto reality and provides the hermeneutical key for obtaining knowledge of it. The BGT accuses revisionism of being a purely philosophical normative ethic because it rejects specifically Christian norms.[8] This statement, however, must be qualified.

Norbert Rigali, S.J., posits a quadripartite division of ethics that many revisionists have found helpful in classifying the specificity of Christian ethics.

> (1) essential morality, incumbent on a person as a member of the human race; (2) existential morality, originating in the individuality of the human person; (3) Christian essential morality, entailed in membership in the Christian community; and (4) Christian existential morality, derived from a person's status as an individual in the Christian fellowship.[9]

Concerning his division, it is important to point out some distinguishing characteristics. Rigali's division includes norms, moral judgments, and the particular *existential context* of those judgments; otherwise (2) and (4) would be redundant for the Christian. Similarly, the decisions that correspond to each division are strictly contextualized within the community to which one belongs, whether it is the universal human community, the Christian community in general, or a specific Christian community.

For example, an "essentialist duty" may entail showing benevolence to one's benefactor. Or a "Christian essentialist" duty may entail a moral responsibility, such as "the duty to witness to Christ," incumbent on a person who belongs to a specific Christian community. "Christian existential" decisions would entail moral responsibilities that a person has as a member of the Christian community such as decisions to become a Catholic priest, join the Jesuits, participate in Eucharist or the sacrament of reconciliation. All such decisions, "if they are authentic, are serious ethical decisions which arise within the context of a Christian community's self-understanding but not outside of it."[10]

One way to perceive Rigali's division is that whereas the two types of essential morality pertain to *duties* or *norms* "incumbent on" a person, the two types of existential morality pertain to the *actual moral judgments* a person makes. From an existentialist perspective, morality is a manifestation of the person's unique identity in a specific context shaped by culture, history, community, and relationships. According to Rigali, "Christian and non-Christian can reach the same moral decision only within the sphere of essential morality."[11] In saying this, it is clear that one does not shed one's Christian identity in making such moral judgments. Rather, the norms that one follows are the same for Christian and non-Christian alike, even though the *meaning* of the moral judgment that one makes in relation to the same essentialist norm may be radically different for the Christian and non-Christian. It is this sphere of morality to which norms belong, according to revisionism. As such, both Christian and non-Christian alike can arrive at these essential norms.

While revisionism would posit the specificity of Christian ethics in the realm of Christian existential moral judgments, and specific Christian norms in the realm of Christian essentialist norms, it would deny that, epistemologically, grace provides any new knowledge in discerning essential norms. According to Josef Fuchs, S.J., "*Even though grace enlightens and strengthens man,* it is the natural *reason* that remains the light of knowledge of the natural law. It is impossible to say when, where and whether God's grace is at work in genuine moral knowledge."[12] While Grisez cites this work, "written before Fuchs became a proportionalist," as "reliable in general,"[13] the BGT would no doubt reject revisionism's assessment of the specificity of Christian ethics. Why is that the case?

According to revisionism, a possible response to this question resides in the definition of "objective" moral order and the epistemological implications for either theory of this order. Essential morality (or ethics) corresponds to this objective order and is distinct from the existential context. For example, while a Jew, Christian, Muslim, and atheist may all follow a norm that "one ought to show benevolence to one's benefactor," they do so in different ways appropriate to the existential context in which the norm applies. For example, a Jew may show benevolence to one's benefactor in a synagogue, a Christian in a church, a Muslim in a mosque, and an atheist in humanitarian organizations. Essential Jewish, Christian, Muslim, or atheistic norms are further specifications of the general norm that "one ought to show benevolence to one's benefactor," and provide the context for fulfilling that norm.

As an ethical theory, revisionism begins with norms accessible to all through the use of reason. There can be universal agreement on general principles of natural law because of an objective moral order. For revisionism, the knowledge of that order that comes from faith is not on the level of essential norms, but on the level of moral judgments. It is within the subjective realm of conscience and the moral judgments that one makes, not the objective realm of norms (objective here would include acts and intentions as these are generically understood, i.e., detached from an *actual* moral judgment), that faith transforms knowledge. The faith in Christ of the individual believer provides what Fuchs refers to as Christian intentionality.[14] This intentionality reflects a specifically Christian perception, motivation, and identity.[15] The specificity of Christian ethics, then, is in the realm of moral judgments that a Christian makes and represents the *further* specification of essential norms that pertain to one's membership in a specific community.

As we have seen, the BGT has a very different definition of the objective realm of morality. Objective morality, and the moral acts that correspond to that morality, "are constituted by what people think they are doing."[16] As stated earlier, there are Christian norms since there are Christian acts. By definition, then, the existential identity of the human person shapes the norms that one follows. Since each individual is unique in his or her individuality, what would limit the description of acts and norms that a Christian follows to Christian acts and norms? What prevents these act and norms from being *more* specific? That is, if there are Christian norms because there are Christian acts, why not further specify these norms? There are Southern Baptist norms because there are Southern Baptist acts. Or, there are John's norms because there are John's acts. It is precisely this subjectivism that the BGT rejects in the realm of normative ethics. By positing the objective realm of morality within the moral agent, however, there is little to prevent such reductionism.

Both the BGT and revisionism would agree that one's Christian commitments shape one's moral judgments so that the moral judgments that a Christian makes, even if they correspond to concrete or essentialist norms, are specific Christian moral judgments. They would further agree that grace provides the strength to fulfill those norms and a perception that may cause an individual to follow another norm (e.g., to forgive one's enemy rather than to seek justice and retribution). They disagree fundamentally, however, on the relationship between revelation and knowledge. For the BGT, Christian norms fulfill natural law norms and provide specific norms not accessible to the non-Christian. One may legitimately ask, then, how natural law is accessible to all through reason? By claiming that Christian norms fulfill and go beyond natural law norms, is the BGT not, in effect, positing two distinct and even incompatible natural laws— one type inclusive and accessible to all human beings, the other exclusive and accessible only to Christians? It seems that revisionism has a more adequate response that maintains the balance between the universality of natural law in the form of material or essential norms while recognizing the specificity of moral judgments for Christians who recognize and follow those norms. The specificity, similar to the BGT, resides in the knowing, willing, and believing subject. However, unlike the BGT, the moral judgments of a Christian do not transform the content of natural law and the norms deduced from it. With these distinctions between the BGT and revisionism in mind, we can proceed to scripture as a source of moral knowledge to see how it functions methodologically in each ethical theory.

Method and Scripture

In utilizing scripture in one's ethical theory one must bear in mind the following two points. First, when investigating the methodological function of scripture in each theory, it is important to recognize that contemporary readers of scripture bring certain presuppositions to the text. These presuppositions, both philosophical and theological, are sometimes neither recognized nor articulated. Part of a methodological investigation of Catholic natural law ethical theory is to bring these presuppositions to the fore in order to comprehend more fully a particular theory.[17] The second point to note is that the attempt to incorporate scripture into one's ethical theory is akin to combining rationally, systematically, and coherently, the full mystery of the reality to which scripture attests, the Triune God of life. This cannot be done, nor is it meant to be. Sacred Scripture, as a collection of books or canon, attempts to reveal the ultimate mystery of existence. This attempt is much more diverse, expansive, and rich than can be grasped by a single system or viewpoint. We must confess humility and approach scripture and our use of it within Christian ethics with great fear and trembling. The fullness of revelation is, and remains, a mystery. The project of developing an ethical theory, however, is not content to live with such a mystery. As a result, there is a fundamental tension between what is contained within scripture and how we use scripture in Christian ethics. Christian ethics will never contain the fullness of revelation, though it can reflect certain dimensions or parts of that revelation that, while no doubt important and foundational, do not tell the whole story. The use of scripture in Christian ethics is similar to the elephant-in-a-dark-room scenario. While every person describes a part of the elephant and is more or less correct in his or her description, no one gives a total description of it. The richness of scripture and the mystery to which it attests defies complete comprehension.

The BGT, Scripture and Method

According to the BGT, the call for the renewal of moral theology at Vatican II requires three components. First, it must be grounded in Sacred Scripture. Second, it must be Christocentric. Third, "moral theology should emphasize both the nobility of the Christian calling and the 'obligation' of Christians 'to bring forth fruit in charity for the life of the world'..." what the BGT calls "the peculiar excellence of the calling to heavenly fulfillment."[18] These three components of renewal express the specific character of Christian ethics that distinguishes it from purely natural law ethics. The justification for each of these claims is grounded in scripture.

The BGT and Scripture

While Grisez, a primary formulator of the BGT, utilizes scripture throughout his contemporary modern-day manual of moral theology, he provides no clearly stated method describing how scripture is being used, asserting only that he "strive[s] only to use Scripture and other witnesses as the Church uses them in her teaching."[19] Although the BGT's deference to church authority *may* be commendable in an ecclesiological sense, this deference may call its scholarly credibility into question as is clear from the church's own limited use of scriptural exegesis in her documents.[20] Following much of the Catholic theological history that focused on Matthew's Gospel, the BGT also relies upon this gospel to "Christianize" the BGT through faith and charity. This is so because, even though Scripture as a whole does not provide concrete answers to all moral questions, Matthew's Gospel "is in a special way the New Testament book of moral teaching."[21] However, since there is no clear methodological explanation of the BGT's use of scripture, we will need to investigate the authority of scripture and *how* it is being used to infer its methodological role and function in the overall theory.

The Authority of Scripture

Establishing the authority of scripture is the point of departure in explaining its function as a source of moral knowledge in the BGT. This is so because scripture provides an essential foundation for the specific content of Christian ethics and the justification for absolute norms derived from the first principle of morality[22] and the Christian modes of response.[23] To establish scripture's authority, it is necessary first to establish the inerrancy of assertions made in the Bible; second, to define an assertion as a proposition that is certainly true and demands assent from those to whom it is directed; and third, on the basis of one and two, to defend the claim that there are assertions proposed in scripture in the form of moral norms that are inerrant moral teachings and, therefore, absolute moral norms. Grisez begins his argument with a quote from Vatican II's *Dei Verbum:*

> Therefore, since everything asserted by the inspired authors or sacred writers must be held to be asserted by the Holy Spirit, it follows that the books of Scripture must be acknowledged as teaching firmly, faithfully, and without error that truth which God wanted put into the sacred writings for the

sake of our salvation. Therefore, "all Scripture is inspired by God and useful for teaching, for reproving, for correcting, for instruction in justice; that the man of God may be perfect, equipped for every good work" (2 Tm 3.16–17…).[24]

While admitting that neither *Dei Verbum* nor Vatican II uses the term *inerrancy* with regard to scripture, the BGT asserts that this is what these and all other church teachings mean when maintaining "everything asserted by the inspired authors is without error."[25] The result of this inerrancy is that "Catholics believe that all propositions asserted in the Bible are true (because God is faithful), believe that the Church as a whole can make no mistake in identifying divine truth, and so work toward an ecclesial understanding of the Bible…."[26]

Key to understanding the Church's position on inerrancy is to define the term *assertion*. "An assertion is a proposition proposed as certainly true."[27] While all assertions in the Bible are held to be certainly true, not everything in the Bible constitutes an assertion. For example, there are different types or genres of literature (poetic, adoration, dialogue) that are not assertions and, therefore, are not inerrant. The challenge of reading scripture, then, is "to determine whether and when the human author is saying, in effect, 'This certainly is true; you ought to believe it.'"[28] Biblical inerrancy applies only to these assertions.

A goal of Christian ethics and its use of scripture, according to the BGT, is to determine what is or is not a moral assertion, and, therefore, a proposition that demands assent. An absolute moral norm in scripture is an asserted proposition that demands assent. The Ten Commandments are a clear example of such asserted propositions. However, not all norms in scripture are assertions. The guide for determining whether or not a norm is an asserted absolute is the church's traditional reading of a particular scriptural text. The church's traditional teaching of, use of, and interpretation of scripture provide the methodological key to how scripture functions in the BGT. In its syllogistic argument for the authority of scripture, the role and function of the magisterium in the BGT is apparent as well.

Use of Scripture: Methodological Considerations

Having established both the authority of scripture and how and on what basis scripture is inerrant, we can look at how the BGT uses scripture. One point must be made initially, however. In the BGT, the attempt to establish inerrancy in scripture is directly related to the claim that there are inerrant, absolute norms contained within scripture. This very line of reasoning reflects the deontological *normative* ethical reasoning that is central to the BGT.[29] This reasoning asserts and justifies absolute norms that forbid certain acts absolutely. Scripture is the source of these norms, either explicitly or implicitly as interpreted by the magisterium.

Revisionist William Spohn notes that there are three important questions to determine one's methodological use of scripture: (1) What scriptural text is selected? (2) How is the text interpreted? and (3) How is it applied to contemporary moral questions?[30] The answers to these questions both reveal the philosophical and theological presuppositions of the author and answer the methodological question of the use of scripture in one's ethical theory.

Selection of Scripture

As noted, the BGT relies heavily upon Matthew's Gospel because it contains much of what scripture has to say about moral teaching.[31] There is a reason that this gospel is often referred to as "the Church's book." Not only is Matthew the only evangelist who uses the Greek term for church *(ekklêsia),*[32] but it also was the predominant gospel in the Catholic Lectionary from Trent until the 1970s. In relying upon Matthew's Beatitudes to provide the scriptural foundation for its theory, the BGT is in agreement with the church's focus on, and selection of, this gospel as well.

For example, in Pope John Paul II's encyclical on the foundations of Christian ethics, *Veritatis Splendor,* the encounter between Jesus and the rich young man (Matt 19:16–22) is the basis for the reflection in Chapter 1 and shapes the entire document. The selection of Matthew's Gospel by the BGT, then, holds strong precedent in church history as well as current magisterial ethical teaching.

Interpretation and Application of Scripture

Intimately related to the selection of scripture is its interpretation and application. One does not select or focus on a text, especially when developing one's ethical theory, without having some preconceived notion of how that text is to be interpreted and applied. Neither ethicists nor biblical exegetes approach the scriptures with a *tabula rasa.* Both bring philosophical and theological presuppositions to their specific interpretations. The BGT's interpretation and application of scripture are intimately related to three concerns of their ethical theory and follow the logical development of that theory. First, the BGT establishes the clear parallels between the basic goods and the affirmation of those goods in scripture. Second, it reveals how the modes of responsibility grounded in these basic goods are transformed through grace and charity into Christian modes of response in and through the Beatitudes. Third, it establishes a specifically Christian natural law theory that contains absolute norms. Matthew's Gospel is the BGT's primary scriptural text for attaining these objectives. The basic goods themselves, however, originate much earlier in scripture.

According to the BGT, the basic goods find their genesis in "Genesis," which "suggests what the basic human goods are."[33] A common aspect shared by the basic goods is harmony. This harmony is disrupted through human disobedience in the Garden of Eden and Cain's slaying Abel. Through Christ and the new covenant, this harmony is restored and, by implication, the basic goods that are a sign of this harmony are reaffirmed. Jesus both loves the basic goods and affirms them in his teachings.[34] This hermeneutic of scripture and its affirmation of the basic goods finds ecclesial support in *Veritatis Splendor.* According to Grisez, what the pope says about the basic goods is consistent with his own position.[35] If one consults Grisez's references to *Veritatis Splendor,* one notes that paragraph 13 explicitly makes a connection between the basic goods, the Ten Commandments, and Jesus' affirmation of them. The encyclical states that "the different commandments of the Decalogue are really only so many reflections of the one commandment about the good of the person, at the level of the many different *goods* which characterize his identity as a spiritual and bodily being in relationship with God, with his neighbour and with the material world."[36] According to the BGT, the basic goods are both reflected in the Decalogue and are asserted in the form of absolute norms.[37]

While all human beings have a natural inclination toward the basic goods, these goods are specified morally by the first principle of morality, which is further specified by the eight modes of responsibility.[38] Christian moral norms, however, cannot be deduced from these modes. "By themselves," they "do not generate the specific norms of Christian morality." In order to do so, "the modes of responsibility must be transformed in the light of faith into modes of Christian response to God's gifts."[39] To that end, the BGT has recourse to the Beatitudes of Matthew's Gospel to transform natural law morality through faith and grace into "key intermediate Christian principles."[40] How does this transformation take place?

> …The modes of Christian response, expressed in summary fashion in the Beatitudes, are the modes of responsibility transformed by faith (which tells us how to live a good life in a fallen world), by hope (which supplies the confidence in God required to make the effort) and by charity (which gives one the power to really live in this way).[41]

The eight modes of responsibility are transformed by the eight Beatitudes into modes of Christian response.[42] Faith gives an insight and knowledge into the ethical order that reason alone cannot grasp, and charity provides the means of following these specifically Christian norms.

Not only do the Beatitudes Christianize the modes of responsibility, but they also provide specific norms of behavior for Christians. This specificity resides in the reality of the human condition transformed through faith. Human beings, though fallen, are redeemed in and through the new covenant personified in Jesus Christ. It is in and through Christ's redemption of humanity that humanity can both *know* the specifically Christian norms that do not contradict, but go beyond purely natural law norms, and *fulfill* those norms through grace.[43]

What, then, are these specifically Christian norms? Grisez claims that "Matthew's Gospel describes Jesus as presenting a strikingly distinctive set of norms, which as a body go beyond anything in the Old Testament as well as in any other religion or philosophy," and provides two examples, forgiveness and love of enemies.[44] The BGT rightly acknowledges that the New Testament does not provide answers to many of the contemporary moral questions confronting humanity. Consequently, it is the church (i.e., magisterium) that provides answers, through its interpretation and application of the moral teachings of scripture, to new moral questions.[45] The absolute moral norms that the magisterium teaches are at the heart of the debate between revisionism and the BGT and include the indissolubility of marriage and the absolute prohibition of the use of artificial birth control, artificial insemination, and masturbation, just to name a few. The BGT clearly recognizes and endorses the church's teaching on these issues, whereas revisionism, while recognizing the premoral values and disvalues that the church is trying to protect or prevent respectively, sees these norms as material, nonabsolute norms.[46]

Christology and Method

Just as one's selection, interpretation, and application of scripture for ethical theory is guided by certain methodological presuppositions, the Christology one derives from scripture and utilizes in one's ethical theory is affected by, and is a reflection of, those presuppositions as well. In a word, our philosophical and theological perspectives function as a hermeneutical key for both scripture and Christology. And while it may be unreasonable to pigeonhole an ethical theory in light of a single Christology, one can certainly discern *Christological tendencies* in both the BGT and revisionism. While the BGT affirms Jesus as "the norm of morality," what, specifically, does this mean? Just as there are many different Christologies,[47] one can have various interpretations of Jesus as norm depending on the Christology espoused. If one focuses on Matthew's Jesus as the New Moses, for example, then the "new law" will be central to understanding who Jesus is and what that means for ethics. If one focuses on Luke's Jesus and its concern for unjust social structures that oppress the poor, then an ethical emphasis on confronting these structures may result. It must be clear that any credible Christology is not an either/or proposition, but a both/and differing in degree and emphasis. This is certainly true with both the BGT and revisionism.

There are at least two senses in which the BGT develops its Christology. The first is through its interpretation of what scripture says about Jesus; the second is by the application of that interpretation to its ethical theory. On the basis of its interpretation of scripture, covenant, incarnation, and the cross are key to the BGT in developing its Christology. The Old Testament prepared the way for the perfection of the first covenant in and through the incarnation. In the incarnation, the human and divine "are inseparably united yet also distinct and not commingled."[48] Consequently, even though Jesus is truly divine, he made a fundamental option to follow the will of God, just as all human beings must do. In so doing, he provided a paradigm for what it means to be authentically human and fully and completely obedient to the will of God. It is this obedience that leads to the cross. Jesus provides the example for human beings to follow and the grace, through the guidance of the Holy Spirit, to follow him.

As an affirmation of its ethical theory, the application of the BGT's Christology presents Jesus as affirming and loving human goods,[49] establishing Christian modes of response in the Sermon on the Mount,[50] teaching absolute moral norms[51] that absolutely prohibit certain acts (e.g., adultery),[52] and refusing to compromise with evil to bring about good.[53] For all practical purposes, it appears that Jesus was the first formulator of the BGT. There is a sense of proof-texting in the BGT's use of scripture to support its theory that is reminiscent of the moral manuals.[54]

There is a curious tension in the BGT's Christology between the use of scripture that shapes and formulates its Christology and its application of that Christology that justifies the BGT itself. What both its use and application share is an emphasis on law, commandment, and obedience to God's will. These are all components that are highlighted in Matthew's Christology. This use and application of scripture finds direct parallels in *Veritatis Splendor.* While Pope John Paul asserts that John's love commandment, "Love one another just as I have loved you" (John 15:12), is the central commandment for Christians,[55] his concern in the encyclical with defending magisterial authority, teaching absolute norms, and rebuffing "teleologism" that challenges the existence of certain absolutes detracts from this central commandment. What is emphasized in the encyclical is the importance of keeping the law and commandments as drawn from Matthew's story of the rich young servant, while neglecting other components of Christology such as Jesus' healings, table fellowship with social outcasts, and the parables that challenge certain moral presuppositions of the time.[56] The deontological and Matthean Christological presuppositions of the encyclical shape the document's Christology and its application to ethics. The same could be said with regard to the BGT. While law, commandment, and obedience are certainly important aspects of Christology and indicate what it means to be a disciple, do these tell the whole, or even the primary, story of Christology? Through its selection, interpretation, and application of scripture and the Christology that it develops from its reading of scripture, certain methodological presuppositions of the BGT are made manifest.

Specificity of Christian Ethics: Methodology, Normative Ethics, and Moral Judgments

For the BGT, both scripture and Christology transform natural law ethics into Christian ethics. The first principle of morality and modes of responsibility (and, one would presume, the basic goods themselves) are transformed through Christian faith and charity. While "the teachings of faith neither conflict with any of the general principles of morality nor add any new principles to them…faith does generate specific norms proper to the Christian life."[57] How does faith do this? "By advancing fresh proposals, faith generates specific norms which could not be known without it."[58] It is the magisterium that formulates those Christian norms. Moral judgments are specifically Christian as well.[59] The BGT's use of scripture and Christology in its ethical theory reflects a deontological normative ethic (there are absolute norms forbidding certain acts absolutely), a supernatural epistemology (faith provides knowledge inaccessible to reason alone), and a hierarchical ecclesiology (it is the role, function, and sole authority of the magisterium to determine the use of scripture in ethics).

Revisionism and Scripture

Whereas the BGT sees scripture as normative and an essential methodological component of its general ethical theory and, in addition, relies upon the Sermon on the Mount to "Christianize" its new natural law, one does not find this centrality of scripture in revisionism's consideration of material norms. Given that revisionism is a natural law Christian ethic as well, why is this not the case? First, although the BGT, as a representative of the faith-ethic school, gives priority to theological ethical method over philosophical ethical method, revisionism gives priority to the latter over the former in developing proportionate reason as a principle for determining right or wrong acts. That does not mean that revelation is not central to revisionism's ethical theory. What it does mean is that this theory is firmly grounded in the natural law tradition that views right reason as humanity's primary source of moral truth, which could be defined in Rigali's classification as essential morality. This truth is accessible to all human beings, not just Christians. For Christians, revelation both confirms the truths derived from reason and serves a specific role in shaping one's perception of reality and motivating one to pursue that truth. This, however, is a distinct realm of ethical discourse, what Rigali refers to as "Christian existential morality."

If indeed scripture does not take on a primary role in constructing revisionism's principle for judging right or wrong acts, what is the role of scripture in the revisionist method? There are two distinct roles. The first pertains to revisionism's philosophical project and justifies the claims of a universal natural law. Thus, revisionism has recourse to Paul's Letter to the Romans. Second, many revisionists accept Bruno Schüller's contention that scripture is concerned primarily with parenesis or exhortation, not normative ethics.[60] While scripture is central to considerations of exhortation, motivation, and perception, its role and function in formulating norms that determine right or wrong acts is negligible. This is clear from the classification of the majority of revisionist moral theologians as belonging to the autonomous ethic school. In Rigali's classification of ethics, this school claims that revelation adds no new essential moral norms to natural law ethics.

Selection of Scripture

Whereas the BGT utilizes Matthew's Sermon on the Mount as its foundational scriptural source and the Beatitudes as a series of moral principles to develop a specifically Christian ethic, revisionism tends to see this sermon as an ideal challenging the Christian to growth and conversion directed toward the kingdom.[61] The tension between these two interpretations of the Beatitudes is reflected in the *Catechism of the Catholic Church* as well. While "the beatitudes confront us with decisive choices concerning earthly goods" (1728), they also "teach us the final end to which God calls us: the Kingdom, the vision of God, participation in the divine nature, eternal life, filiation, rest in God" (1726).[62] Depending on whether one focuses on the "already" or "not yet" of the kingdom of God will determine, in part, which perception of the Beatitudes one adopts. The eschatological focus of either theory in relation to the Beatitudes is clear.

Rather than pursuing a specifically Christian normative ethic grounded in the Beatitudes, revisionism relies upon Paul's Letter to the Romans to ground its humanistic and empirical approach to ethics. The first two chapters of this epistle provide the traditional foundation for natural law theology.[63] While St. Paul by no means is portrayed by revisionism as establishing, let alone defending, a natural law ethic, what he proposes is a vision of an orderly universe created by God that is conducive to such an ethic (Rom 1:18–20) and human awareness or knowledge of the (natural) law that is part of human nature (Rom 2:12–15). Schüller summarizes the relationship between natural law and the first two chapters of Romans: "If by natural law is understood the totality of ethical norms that can be known at least in principle in logical independence of Scripture, then the Epistle to the Romans offers proof that such a natural law actually exists."[64] While the BGT uses scripture exclusively to highlight the specificity of Christian ethics, revisionism uses scripture inclusively to highlight the universality of the natural law.[65]

Interpretation and Application of Scripture

Revisionism interprets and applies these chapters from Romans based on certain philosophical and theological ethical methodological presuppositions that it brings to the text. The first interpretation and application is dependent upon philosophical ethical method and epistemology. We come to know the truths of natural law in two ways. The first is through empirical observation: "Ever since the creation of the world his invisible nature, namely his eternal power and deity, has been clearly perceived in the things that have been made" (Rom 1:20). One can discern the objective truths of natural law in and through the created universe, independently of revelation. Second, we intuit these truths: "What the law requires is written on [our] hearts" (Rom 2:15). God created human beings in such a way that, regardless of religious beliefs, a common human nature allows us to know the objective truths of natural law. These interpretations of the passages in Romans support the humanistic natural law ethic of revisionism. Josef Fuchs, S.J., while affirming St. Paul's defense of natural law in Romans,[66] draws a clear line of demarcation between reason and revelation. "Human reason can attain a natural knowledge of the natural law independently of revelation and our knowledge of the fundamental moral principles can justly be described as easy of acquisition."[67] Nevertheless, revelation facilitates reason's ability to discern these truths.[68]

The second revisionist interpretation of this text focuses on the overall theological meaning of the first three chapters of Romans for Christians. An essential theological point is that sin has affected all human perceptions and, therefore, all are in need of Christ's salvific love and redemption. Theologically, this insight has implications for a philosophical natural law ethic. The reality of sin and its ability to distort perception *can* limit reason's ability to know the natural law. As is clear from history and from Pope John Paul's public apologies to the world regarding the behavior of the church's faithful in the past,[69] human beings are not exempt from the power of sin to distort the faculty of reason. In spite of this, however, reason by its very nature has the capacity to know the dictates of natural law, though the grace of revelation through scripture and tradition certainly facilitates this knowledge.

The distinction between the philosophical and the theological interpretation and application of scripture reflects the overarching methodological significance of scripture for revisionism. While the BGT endorses scripture as providing the very *foundation* of a specifically Christian natural law ethic as this has been handed down and interpreted by tradition through the magisterium's authority, revisionism proposes scripture as a *confirmation* of natural law.

Christology and Method

Not surprisingly, the Christologies of the two theories differ as well. While the BGT proposes a Christology based on Matthew's Gospel that sees the incarnation as a radical transformation of what has come before and, further, as the inauguration of a new and specific moral law, revisionism has a different perspective. Revisionism prefers the Christology developed in John's Gospel, both philosophically as it confirms the universality of the natural law, and theologically as it highlights the specificity of Christian ethics. Philosophically, the Gospel according to St. John describes the Word, or *Logos,* from the beginning as one with God (John 1:1–18). While this Christology "from above" or "descending Christology" is frequently identified with the pre-Vatican II church,[70] it does have significant implications for revisionism's philosophical stance on natural law. The rationale for opting for John's *Logos* Christology follows directly from revisionism's vision of natural law. If God created an orderly universe and Jesus was with God from the beginning, then the incarnation is the concrete manifestation and radical affirmation of this order. This in no way negates the importance of the life, death, and resurrection of

Jesus. It merely confirms that which has always been, namely, an orderly universe created by God from the beginning that reveals the entirety of moral truth. As Ephesians and Colossians attest, not only is Christ the affirmation of this order but also, in fact, "in him and for him all things were created."[71] Whereas the BGT sees the incarnation as a *radical transformation* from what has come before, revisionism views it as a continuation and *radical confirmation* of what has already been promised from the beginning.

Theologically, John's Gospel contains the specifically Christian principle of Christian ethics that is grounded in Jesus. "I give you a new commandment: Love one another. Such as my love has been for you, so must your love be for each other. This is how all will know you for my disciples: your love for one another" (John 13:34–35). As William Spohn notes, this "new commandment has a distinctive reference to the person of Jesus that is not found in the two great commandments to love God and neighbor."[72] The words and deeds of Jesus are the paradigm for what it means to be authentically human for Christians. Jesus is the concrete universal norm.[73] It is through striving to follow Jesus by the grace provided through the Holy Spirit that humans are enabled to live according to the dictates of natural law. For revisionism, it is this grace and the motivation provided in scripture that manifests the specific nature of Christian ethics. This specificity, however, belongs to the human person, Christian existential morality, and *actual* moral judgments, not to essential normative content and the right or wrong acts that it prescribes or prohibits.

Specificity of Christian Ethics: Moral Judgments

Many revisionists recognize a distinction between normative ethics and parenesis when it comes to scripture as a source for Christian ethics.[74] Whereas normative ethics is concerned with content, parenesis exhorts or provides "Christian intentionality"[75] to fulfill that which is already known through reason. For revisionism, natural law is universal. What is specific to Christian ethics is the motivation for a Christian to follow natural law norms. Some philosophers and theologians have criticized the distinction between Christian intentionality and autonomous moral content as too superficial because the motivation or reason for an act frequently enters into the very meaning or content of the act.[76] As Vincent MacNamara notes, for instance, "Christianity may indeed give the desire for virginity. But basically, it gives one the reason why virginity is a morally good choice. Without the considerations arising from Christian belief, it might not be an intelligible choice."[77] In this way, although people may ostensibly do the same act, the act itself is fundamentally different because of the reasons or motivation for acting and the meaning of the act itself. If this is the case, then, by positing parenesis as the specifically Christian component of Christian ethics, what revisionism is claiming by implication is that there *is* a specific Christian content both in moral judgments and norms. Commenting on Fuchs's "Christian intentionality," Grisez would concur with MacNamara. "[Fuchs] fails to see that acts with different intelligible content, even if they are behaviorally the same, are different moral acts. Thus he misses the impact of a Christian 'intentionality,' displacing it into the mysterious realm of fundamental freedom. He also thinks of moral norms as if they were a limited set of available rules."[78] MacNamara and Grisez's criticisms warrant closer investigation.

Normative Ethics and Moral Judgments

As we discussed in the Introduction, there are various levels of ethical discourse. These various levels may facilitate clarity and the formulation of an adequate response to those who challenge the parenesis hypothesis as merely substantiating a specifically Christian ethic. Actual moral judgments are distinct from normative ethics. These judgments entail the day-to-day decisions that human beings make. Normative ethics are reflections on these moral judgments that attempt to provide a foundation and formulation of norms of behavior to guide moral judgments.

For example, two people of different cultural and religious backgrounds may pay their taxes. In so doing, they are following a norm: It is right to pay taxes. Furthermore, the specific motivation for each may be to be a good citizen. Nonetheless, the *meaning* of the act for each individual may be profoundly different. A Christian living in a capitalist society might see her act as fulfilling the gospel mandate, "Give to Caesar what is Caesar's." An atheist living in the former Soviet Union might see his act as fulfilling his civic duties and responsibilities as a patriot. Would we say, as does MacNamarra[79] and the BGT,[80] that these are two different acts? We may respond yes *and* no. Yes, in the sense that, for each person, each and every *actual* moral judgment is a unique manifestation of who he or she is, as a person. These are also the same acts, however, in the sense that both the act (paying taxes) and reason for the act (to fulfill one's religious and/or social responsibilities) are the same. Certainly the question of the meaning of the act raises the importance of developing a thorough understanding of the human act and its relationship to normative ethics.

We can glean some insight into the relationship between norms and moral judgments from Louis Janssens' personalist criterion, especially his eighth dimension: "All human persons are fundamentally equal, but at the same time each is an originality."[81] Janssens goes on to explain how these two dimensions manifest themselves in norms and behavior. "Equality and originality imply that all must let their activity be guided by the universal prescriptions of morality and that at the same time each one must bring his originality to expression through his behavior."[82] The anthropological ethical assertion that every human being is a unique originality substantiates the claim that every actual moral judgment is a concrete expression of that unique originality, including Christian intentionality, with the history, culture, values, responsibilities, relationships, and perceptions that an individual expresses in and through moral judgments. From an historically conscious perspective, the concrete person in history is normative.[83] This normativity, however, is manifested in actual moral decisions or judgments, not normative content. Universal prescriptions of morality belong to the realm of normative ethics and are general norms that either prescribe or prohibit certain acts and/or motivations. These norms become incarnated in and through the actual moral judgments of a unique human person. There is, then, an important distinction between norms or normative content and the *possible* moral judgments they prescribe or prohibit and *actual* moral judgments. The former belong to an objective moral order and function as general guidelines for human beings, whereas the latter are a unique manifestation of the individual and his or her application of the norm in light of the social, cultural, relational, and communal dimensions in which that individual exists. Another way of formulating this relationship is that whereas norms pertain to the objective realm, moral judgments manifest the subjective realm, including Christian intentionality and one's fundamental freedom, and have an impact on the objective realm. Normative ethics, even when it includes synthetic norms, reflects the objective realm to the extent that it is neither the role nor function of a norm to encapsulate the total meaning of an act for a human person. Since the BGT does not distinguish between these two realms in moral judgments, their normative ethic entails both dimensions. That is why the BGT can assert, "There are specifically Christian norms because there are specifically Christian acts."[84]

For revisionism, then, to assert that scripture is parenetical rather than normative ethical does not, by implication, create a specifically Christian *normative* ethic. It does, however, certainly recognize that, on the level of actual moral judgments, the meaning of actions for an individual is unique to that individual and represents a concrete manifestation of her relationships, culture, commitments, values, ideals, and religious beliefs. This I have referred to elsewhere as the human act adequately considered.[85] It is a view of the human act that is distinct from the endeavor of normative ethics. In this sense, then, revisionism certainly espouses a specifically Christian component of ethical discourse.

This component, however, belongs to moral judgments and parenesis, not to the formulation of norms prescribing or prohibiting right or wrong acts.

Specificity and Christian Ethics: Perception, Identity, and Motivation

Recently, William Spohn has reshaped the question of the specificity of Christian ethics and, in so doing, has argued that the Jesus narrative is normative for Christian ethics. This normativity is manifested in perception, motivation, and identity. Before any discussion of the foundation and components of his thesis, it is important to understand why the debate on the specificity of Christian ethics came to a dead end.

> [The debate] concentrated on the *what* of morality to the exclusion of the *how*. The debate got muddled by asking what principles or values obligated Christians that obligated no one else. Since the autonomy school sharply distinguished motive from moral content, it relegated Scripture to providing affective backing to common human values and obligations.... Scripture primarily exerts its normative function by setting a pattern of dispositions rather than dictating directly the content of action. These dispositions (the *how* of morality) then guide the agent to discern *what* to do or forego.[86]

Spohn affirms MacNamara's and, by implication, Grisez's assertion that "why and how we act enters into the moral meaning of what we do."[87] Spohn's proposal confirms Fuchs's "Christian intentionality," yet attempts to integrate this "with distinctive ways of behavior that are both Christian and humane." The means of attaining this synthesis are through the "analogical imagination."[88]

The analogical imagination posits Jesus' story as the paradigm for what it means to be authentically human for Christians. Analogy establishes continuity between this story and the current lived experience of the Christian and looks for familiar patterns in new circumstances. Imagination enables one to discern who to become and what to do in light of these patterns. In this way, then, Jesus is normative for Christian ethics as a "concrete universal." "His particular story embodies a paradigmatic pattern which has a universal moral applicability....Christians move imaginatively from his story to their new situation by analogical reasoning."[89] The impact of the concrete universal is evident in three dimensions of moral experience: perception, motivation, and identity.[90]

Jesus as a concrete universal shapes our perception of reality. The Christian narrative functions as a lens through which we perceive reality. In fact, this perception establishes interpretive patterns or *gestalts* on many different levels. It affects the individual Christian in moral judgments, the biblical scholar in discerning a "canon within a canon," a Christian ethicist in interpreting scripture and extrapolating the central meaning of scripture with regard to ethics, and Christian institutions in their commitments. In the case of a Christian and his particular moral judgments, this lens enables him both to see the morally significant features of an act and to make a moral judgment in light of that perception. For example, Christian perception might cause a person to choose to forgive rather than to seek just retribution.

Second, Jesus as the concrete universal "indicates *how* to act even when his story does not directly indicate *what* to do."[91] Scripture has its main impact on the imagination and motivation. Through this impact, we discern paradigms that become "scenarios for action." These paradigms become practical in two stages. "First, they contain a discernible pattern which can be noticed elsewhere. Second, there are procedures for extending the paradigm to new situations."[92] As our faith and life of holiness mature, so too does their impact on *how* to act (i.e., motive grounded in Christian agape) and on *what we choose* when we act. As scripture testifies and nature affirms, a good tree bears good fruit. The more mature the vine, the fuller the wine.

The maturation of Christian motivation shapes our very identity and "*who* we are to become as Christians, individually and communally,"[93] the third impact of Jesus as the concrete universal. (This perception of identity has close parallels to the BGT that sees the Christian life as an unfolding vocation shaped by the cumulative process of the choices and moral judgments that we make.)[94] Analogously (pardon the pun) for Spohn, individual moral judgments must be seen in the broader context of a personal narrative that "forms the normative basis of personal identity."[95] Just as all the individual stories of Jesus and various forms or genres of literature (e.g., parables, healing stories, table fellowship) that depict his life are held together by a single narrative, so too our stories (made up of experiences, choices, and motivations) are united by our personal narrative. Through analogy, the lives of Christians parallel the life of Jesus in and through his redemptive love. In positing Christian identity as a central dimension of Jesus as concrete universal, Spohn finds a solid basis for such a claim in the work of narrative ethicists such as Stanley Hauerwas.[96]

Conclusion

What is to be said of Spohn's proposal in light of the specificity of Christian ethics and the comparison between revisionism and the BGT and their use of scripture? First, Spohn's perception of scripture and the analogical imagination could be a source for common ground between the two ethical theories. Certainly the BGT is committed to drawing out the full implications of scripture and Christology for ethics. However, in the common ground lie the trenches as well. The relative gestalts of each ethical theory in approaching scripture dictate against such common ground. Whereas the BGT is committed to articulating and defending moral absolutes, revisionism as a theological ethic is more concerned with the meaning of acts for human persons and how those acts either facilitate or frustrate authentic personhood in light of the gospel. While the BGT would accept this emphasis in theory, it would maintain that certain acts, by definition, fundamentally frustrate authentic personhood. This brings us back to the basic methodological divisions between the two theories that we have already discussed.

Second, positing Jesus as a concrete universal certainly highlights the specificity of Christian ethics and reflects the BGT's own theological project. The transformation of the human person through Christian faith and charity in perception, motivation, and identity are included in the BGT. Whereas Spohn, as do many revisionist moral theologians, posits virtue ethics and character ethics as the realm in which the specificity of Christian ethics should be developed, the BGT sees these approaches as inadequate. Contrary to much of the Christian tradition (especially in the work of Aquinas) that focuses on the importance of the virtues, the BGT instead proposes "an ethics of personal vocation" that "more intelligibly and fruitfully views Christian life as an ordered whole."[97] The role and function of virtue in vocation would be the topic of an interesting study. Common to both proposals is the focus on the person and how human acts shape the identity of the person. In fact, Spohn's development of a theological anthropology is the very locus of resolution that Jean Porter,[98] among others,[99] has posited as a possible resolution to, or at least peaceful coexistence between, what appears to be the interminableness of the debate between the two ethical theories.

Finally, in relation to Fuchs and criticisms leveled against him by MacNamara and Grisez, it is not clear to me that Spohn's attempt to refine "Christian intentionality" by reuniting the act and agent has resolved the tension or substantially moved beyond what has been at the core of the debate between the two schools of thought. The three realms that Spohn posits in relation to Jesus as the concrete universal (perception, motivation, and identity) all belong to the moral agent, and thus to the subjective realm of morality. In relation to Rigali's division, it seems that Spohn is addressing primarily the Christian essentialist (normative) and Christian existentialist (moral judgments) ethical realms while leaving the objective or essentialist realm of morality largely intact.

As I understand him, Spohn's contribution is to develop a theological anthropology and specifically to articulate *how* Jesus functions as a concrete universal in shaping the subjective dimensions of the human person. To what extent, however, does this impact the analysis of the objective rightness or wrongness of acts? The bridge between the two, act and agent, objective and subjective, right and good, essentialist and Christian essentialism and existentialism, would lie in perception. Christian perception highlights certain features of a situation that are morally significant based on the Christian story and analogical imagination, but it also does so in light of "human nature, practical effectiveness, accurate descriptions of data, and the accumulated wisdom of the tradition."[100] It seems to me that Fuchs' assertion with regard to grace and the inability to determine its impact on our knowledge of the natural law would apply to Christian perception as well. To what extent has the challenge to traditional Catholic teachings—slavery, for example, and more recently capital punishment—been grounded in reason as compared to revelation? Is one more likely to find resolution to the birth control debate in Catholic moral theology through reason, experience, and science or through revelation, scripture, and tradition? While the impact of scripture on our knowledge and development of norms may be difficult to determine, it certainly has a role in the actual moral judgments that Christians make. In the methodological use of scripture in ethical theory, both the BGT and revisionism could agree on this point.

While Jesus as concrete universal norm and the other three grounds for moral reflection that Spohn mentions (human nature, practical effectiveness, accurate descriptions of data) highlight the necessary complimentarity between reason and revelation, it is the fourth source of moral knowledge (tradition) that is at the heart of the debate between the BGT and revisionism. What constitutes "the accumulated wisdom of the tradition" radically differentiates the two theories and largely determines the hermeneutic of all the other sources of moral knowledge. It is this final source of moral knowledge that we shall now address.[101]

4
Tradition and Method

In the Introduction we noted two senses of tradition as a source of moral knowledge. Tradition with a capital "T" depicts the infrastructure and process or system for handing over lived faith, and tradition with a small "t" is the content of that lived faith that is handed over. The impacts of Tradition and tradition on moral theology are extensive and warrant far greater treatment than we can do them justice in a single chapter. Consequently, we must narrow our methodological investigation to three central issues. First, what is the nature of the relationship between theologians and the magisterium; second, what are the criteria for determining whether or not moral teachings belonging to the "secondary object of infallibility" have been taught infallibly; and third, intrinsically linked to this second issue, which, if any, norms belong to the "secondary object of infallibility"? The first issue pertains to Tradition whereas the latter two issues pertain to tradition. The differences in ecclesiological models between the BGT and revisionism provide the key for understanding and responding to these questions. In this chapter, we will address these questions after briefly describing the position of each theory on the nature of the magisterium (Tradition), the authority of its teachings (tradition), and ecclesiology. We will then conclude with a brief overview of the two theories and possible common ground for future dialogue between them.

"Tradition" and "tradition"

It is only relatively recent that the teaching authority of the Catholic Church has been identified with the "magisterium."[1] In contemporary usage, *magisterium* refers to the pastoral teaching authority of the church on "faith and morals" as the bishops and Roman Pontiff exercise it. Being stewards of the Holy Spirit, those in authority do not create truth, but are searchers and revealers of meaning as it is discovered and articulated as truth. The magisterium is commonly referred to as either extraordinary or ordinary. The extraordinary magisterium is exercised in two ways. First, as defined by Vatican I's *Pastor Aeternus,* when the Roman Pontiff speaks *ex cathedra,* such statements possess the infallibility with which the divine Redeemer willed his church to be endowed in defining doctrine concerning faith or morals.[2] The second exercise of the extraordinary magisterium occurs in council where bishops and pope in union profess "solemn judgments" defining doctrines of faith.[3] In both of these cases, the defined doctrines are infallible. That is, they are irreformable doctrines whose truth is guaranteed by the guidance of the Holy Spirit, and they require the faithful's religious assent that is absolute and certain.[4] Such weight is given to infallible teachings within the entire Catholic community that the exercise of this teaching authority is extremely rare.[5]

The ordinary universal magisterium is the day-to-day exercise of the bishop's pastoral teaching mission throughout the world, including papal encyclicals.[6] Theologically speaking, the teachings of the ordinary magisterium can also be infallible when, as we shall see below, certain conditions are fulfilled.

The magisterium can issue two different types of infallible teachings as well as noninfallible teachings. The first type of infallible teaching is described as belonging to the "primary object of infallibility" and is limited to those doctrines that represent the deposit of revelation, i.e., they are divinely revealed. The second type is described as belonging to the "secondary object of infallibility."[7] While these teachings are not divinely revealed, they are so intimately linked to, and represent a necessary expression of, divine revelation that the magisterium may define them infallibly. By contrast, noninfallible teachings are those teachings that, while admitting of the possibility of reevaluation and redefinition in light of changing historical circumstances, further scientific developments, or deeper theological investigation and reflection, at the present time reflect an authoritative position of the magisterium that must be given "religious respect,"[8] i.e., such teachings warrant a presumption of truth among the faithful. Nevertheless, such teachings can be erroneous. Both the BGT and revisionism recognize the authority of the ordinary and extraordinary magisterium to teach infallibly on faith and morals. The locus of their disagreement is whether the ordinary universal magisterium has taught specific natural law norms infallibly. The respective ecclesiologies of each theory shape the hermeneutical lens for interpreting the criteria laid down by the magisterium itself to determine whether the conditions to declare such norms infallible have been fulfilled.

Ecclesiology and Tradition

The late Richard McCormick, S.J., frequently pointed out that one's understanding of the teaching authority on morality within the church is intimately linked with one's ecclesiology, or understanding of the church.[9] The BGT recognizes the fundamental importance of this relationship as well.[10] Ecclesiology is central to how one comprehends Tradition and the role and function of the magisterium in relation to the theologian and the faithful.

Since Vatican II, theologians have generally adhered to two fundamentally different ecclesiological models. The model that originated in the Middle Ages and predominated up until Vatican II is the hierarchical model. According to this ecclesiological model, knowledge flows downward from the magisterium to theologians to the faithful. The role and function of theologians in this model is to explain and clarify to the faithful what the magisterium has taught authoritatively, but not to question or challenge those teachings.[11] While the *sensus fidelium* (sense of the faithful) and their experiences are a source for informing the magisterium in its formulation of moral doctrines, it is the magisterium's responsibility to determine how that experience is to be interpreted and incorporated into its teaching. In cases where there is a disparity between human experience and magisterial teaching (e.g., artificial birth control), the magisterium holds the trump card. According to this model, then, the magisterium is the final authority for interpreting, formulating, and dispensing moral truth. Theologians help to explain and disseminate that truth to the faithful. They should not question or challenge authoritative, noninfallible teachings where the magisterium has deliberately stated an opinion about a controverted matter, even if their scholarship challenges it, but should defend and explain such teachings. If we think of this ecclesiological model as a pyramid, the magisterium is at the pinnacle of the pyramid and is the hermeneutical key for all other sources of moral knowledge.

With Vatican II came a profound transition in ecclesiology and, by implication, moral epistemology. The proposed concentric model is referred to as the people of God or *communio* (communion) model.[12] Within this model, knowledge is discerned through the people of God in its entirety—the magisterium, theologians, and the faithful alike. There is a "trialogue," if you will, among the three groups guided by the Holy Spirit with scripture and human experience at the very center of this conversation. It is this ongoing conversation that moves the pilgrim church through history toward a fuller recognition, knowledge, understanding, and appreciation of God's self-communication to humanity. While the magisterium still maintains authority in this model, and there is a presumption of truth regarding its teaching, this authority is qualified by its role as learner-teacher. The faithful and theologians facilitate, contribute to, and sometimes may even challenge noninfallible magisterial teachings in this learning-teaching process.

The BGT espouses a hierarchical ecclesiology. Grisez and Shaw note, "God prescribes that there be a visible human community which is 'the Church' and that it be organized hierarchically rather than democratically or in some other way."[13] Within such a model, hierarchical authority, and obedience and conformity to that authority, are key. While the BGT recognizes the importance of the contributions of both theologians and the faithful in this model, how does it explain their respective roles in relation to the magisterium? It is the task of theologians to aid the magisterium by eliciting "the testimony of witnesses of faith on matters about which the magisterium must judge" and to propose "the material or conceptual content for possible judgments by which the faith will be freshly articulated and developed, or challenges to it answered." In addition, "the faithful at large can propose material from their experience."[14] What happens if the experiences of the faithful conflict with the authoritative judgments of the magisterium? "A sound method in moral theology will not allow the moral experiences and judgments of some of the contemporary faithful to override the constant and very firm moral teaching of the Church."[15] In this case, it is the role of the theologian to consult moral principles and the fundamental truths of faith "to find resources for explaining modern experience and criticizing dissenting opinions."[16] What if theologians find grounds for legitimate dissent from noninfallible magisterial teachings based on the experiences of the faithful and/or their own research and scholarship? While rational argumentation can sometimes be convincing, it is susceptible to distorting the truth, according to the BGT. "No moral theory can settle any issue with complete certainty by experience and purely rational analysis."[17] The only possibility for legitimate dissent from noninfallible moral norms is if a stronger authority is drawn from faith itself. Since it is the ultimate authority of the magisterium to interpret articles of faith, the hierarchical epistemological circle is complete. That is, the magisterium issues teachings on faith and morals, and theologians defend those teachings. If theologians are to have a legitimate basis to question noninfallible teachings, they must invoke a higher source drawn from faith itself "such as Scripture, a defined doctrine, or a teaching proposed infallibly by the ordinary magisterium."[18] The magisterium is responsible for interpreting and defining sources of faith. Given the constraints for legitimate dissent from noninfallible magisterial teaching, such dissent is very limited in this ecclesiological model.

Contrarily, revisionism espouses a people of God or communion ecclesiological model. This model is based on trinitarian theology in that, just as the Trinity is a relational entity, no member superior to the other, so too the three bodies that constitute the church.[19] While this model does not deny the importance and authority of the magisterium as an authoritative witness to truth, it stands in relation to, not above, the other two bodies. The relationship between the magisterium, theologians, and the people of God is communal and dialectical. It is communal in the sense that *all* the faithful share a common baptism that unites them in faith. On the basis of this faith, the faithful "cannot err in matters of belief."[20] Given this communal unity, however, there remain different gifts and roles in discovering, articulating, and defining "matters of belief." For the faithful, experience in their faith journey as this is lived out and manifested in community is key to determining what constitutes matters of belief. For moral theologians, it is reflection on that experience as well as upon revelation and reason that helps to formulate and articulate matters of belief in a comprehensive ethical system. For the magisterium, it is discernment that both listens to the experiences of the faithful and is in thoughtful, honest, and respectful dialogue with theologians in the process of formulating matters of belief and teaching authoritatively. In all of these processes, the Holy Spirit is present to guide the entire church. Whenever there is a disagreement over noninfallible magisterial teachings, whether it be the faithful in relation to the magisterium, theologians in relation to the magisterium, or the magisterium in relation to the faithful and theologians, such disagreements must be thoroughly investigated to discern their source, their validity, and if and how it challenges those teachings. Mere disagreement does not constitute an argument against noninfallible teachings. What it does warrant is a serious investigation that can seek to clarify, correct, or in extreme cases change those teachings on the basis of responsible dialogue. The only teachings that are beyond these considerations are infallible teachings.

Both of these ecclesiological models are evident in the early history of the church and can be defended through recourse to the documents of Vatican II. Historically, Francis Sullivan notes that whereas the roots of the infallibility of ecumenical councils and popes date back to the ninth and thirteenth centuries respectively, "the conviction that the consensus of the universal church in its faith is an infallible norm of truth goes back to the second century, with Irenaeus, and is a consistent element of Christian belief."[21] Grisez challenges this revisionist perspective on history and authority within the church. Instead, he defends the kind of teaching authority the hierarchy claims for itself in *Lumen Gentium* 25 and *Dei Verbum* 10 as stemming back to Jesus' authorizing the apostles to teach with authority. He writes, "The fact that supreme teaching authority, *however exercised and articulated,* is vested in the pope and bishops as successors of the apostles goes back to the origin of the Church herself."[22] Furthermore, support for both models can be deduced from Vatican II's documents, especially *Lumen Gentium,* depending on one's interpretive lens. In fact, there is a dialectic between the ecclesiological model one espouses, the documents of Vatican II, and the hermeneutical lens one develops in order to interpret those documents. Revisionism interprets those documents as expressing ecclesiological innovations that departed significantly from the ecclesiology developed in the Middle Ages, and that continued up until Vatican II. Avery Dulles refers to this perspective as a "hermeneutics of discontinuity."[23] The BGT would opt for a hermeneutics of continuity whereby Vatican II merely reaffirmed the traditional hierarchical ecclesiology.[24]

As I understand the debate over the hierarchy and its teaching authority, the important question is not *if* the bishops and pope have this teaching authority, but *how* the teaching authority is to be exercised. That is the very point of debate on the historical investigation of ecclesiological models. Whereas the BGT has a very limited role for the faithful and theologians in their hierarchical model, revisionism's people of God model allows for much greater input from both groups in developing, formulating, and reformulating noninfallible teachings. This model is particularly relevant for the contemporary church, given that many of the faithful are educated and have a very active ministry within church institutions (e.g., universities and parishes). Furthermore, with the radical decline of vocations to the priesthood and religious life in the contemporary church, the church herself is moving more toward a "Church of the Laity" whereby the laity have a much greater role to play in every aspect of church life. For revisionism, the repositioning of authority based on a revised, yet traditional, ecclesiology reflects not only a trinitarian theology and the documents of Vatican II but also Catholic social teaching and the principle of subsidiarity or participation that applies to social and ecclesial structures.[25] The implications of these sources for the authority of the magisterium and its relationship to theologians and the faithful supports a communion ecclesiological model that is more reflective of the "signs of the times" than is the antiquated exclusively hierarchical model.

In light of these two different ecclesiological models, we can now address three central issues concerning the teaching authority of the magisterium on morality and its role and function within ethical theory that divide the BGT and revisionism. The first issue is the proper relationship between theologians and the magisterium when the magisterium exercises its teaching function.

Relationship Between Theologians and the Magisterium

The BGT and the Juridical Model

At the heart of the current "crisis of faith in the Church"[26] according to Grisez, is the "cancer" of dissenting theologians.[27] This state of affairs is due, in large part, to an improper relationship between the magisterium (pope and bishops) and theologians in the magisterial process. To heal this cancer, Grisez proposes a juridical or high court model for this relationship that follows from a hierarchical ecclesiological model.[28] There are three features to this "high court" model. "The pope and other bishops should first listen together to theological debate, then dismiss the theologians and engage in their own reflection."[29] In this way, the role and function of theologians in relation to the magisterium becomes clear. Just as the arguments of the advocates representing each side of a case settle nothing, so too this model "would make clear to everyone the quite limited and relative value of all theological arguments."[30] The act of evaluating and judging those arguments is reserved for the magisterium "in chambers." Second, "Theologians and others invited to make their appropriate contributions to the theological debate should be instructed clearly regarding what is expected of them."[31] In the case of disputed theological viewpoints, "both sides should be given equal and adequate opportunities to present their cases."[32] Finally, "To assure collegial solidarity in magisterial judgments, those which concern disputed questions ordinarily should be made in a collegial manner as the outcome of such a process."[33]

Grisez's high court analogy does not end with the magisterial process of judgment but reflects what may be considered a punitive component for dissenting theologians as well. Grisez belittles the 1985 assembly of the Synod of Bishops' call for "reciprocal dialogue between the bishops and theologians...for the building up of the faith and its deeper comprehension"[34] given the current state of "radical dissent" within the Catholic Church.

Instead, he proposes the remedies of the first assembly of the synod in 1967. "Those who are rash or imprudent should be warned in all charity; those who are pertinacious should be removed from office."[35]

This juridical model is based on certain premises. First, the magisterium "should respect" the scholarly authority of theologians.[36] Second, rational arguments do not carry doctrinal weight.[37] Third, the special sacramental power of popes and bishops, through grace, gives them supernatural access to truth.[38] Fourth, while recognizing that the magisterium can err in authoritative, noninfallible teachings, these teachings ought to be followed because "even when it is not clear that the bishop's or pope's teaching is proposed infallibly, one has a good reason for assuming that his teaching pertains to divine revelation."[39]

Fifth, the juridical model is based on a hierarchical ecclesiology represented, for example, in *Humani Generis* and *Lumen Gentium* 25. There is a curious tension here between the BGT reliance upon *Humani Generis* to defend the proper relationship between the magisterium and theologians and Grisez's critique of this relationship prior to Vatican II. As he notes, "Before Vatican II, too much conformity was demanded of Catholic theologians. Their work was so closely integrated with the magisterium's work that there was virtually no room for them to propose views which the magisterium could not at once accept and approve."[40] Revisionism would certainly agree with this statement. Furthermore, revisionism would posit the statements of *Humani Generis* used by Grisez to defend his juridical model as both a reflection and confirmation of this unhealthy relationship.

Finally, material for debate in this model presumes issues open to discussion. The reliance upon, and authority granted to, Pius XII's *Humani Generis* substantially limits this material. Pius XII declares, "But if the Supreme Pontiffs in their acts, after due consideration, express an opinion on a hitherto controversial matter, it is clear to all that this matter, according to the mind and will of the same Pontiffs, cannot any longer be considered a question of free discussion among the theologians."[41] This statement applies to noninfallible pronouncements and is sometimes expressed in the Latin aphorism, *Roma locuta, causa finita.* As we shall see below, this last premise is intimately linked to the debate over what belongs to the secondary object of infallibility.

Revisionism and the Dialogical Model

Revisionism qualifies or rejects these premises, rejecting also the BGT's high court or juridical model. Instead, revisionism posits a dialogical model for the relationship between theologians and the magisterium. Revisionism's response to the BGT's premises focuses first on the term *respect.* Respect should entail not only allowing theologians to present their arguments, but also the magisterium's seriously and accurately considering the content and meaning of those arguments without an inherent bias in favor of those theologians who merely support a traditional, noninfallible, position. As it stands, and as *Veritatis Splendor's* misrepresentation of proportionalism made evident,[42] there is a magisterial presupposition against revisionism that makes such respect and unbiased appraisal of arguments problematic in the current situation. Second, given that rational arguments are not a *sufficient* criterion for determining and formulating authoritative, noninfallible teaching, they are certainly a *necessary* criterion. When there are sound reasons and arguments for challenging what may, by definition, be an erroneous teaching, those arguments should be given due consideration. How those arguments relate to, and utilize, other sources of moral knowledge must be analyzed and discussed in their entirety.

Third, given the accessibility to the truths of natural law through right reason, revisionism would qualify the BGT's epistemological claim concerning the relationship between knowledge and grace. Certainly God's grace, as promised to the church and in a special way to the magisterium, facilitates the process in the discernment of truth, but it does not dispense the church from the very human tasks of gathering information and evaluating that information.[43] It is in this process that the development of moral doctrine takes place, as history has shown.[44]

Fourth, revisionism would accuse the BGT of advocating a certain "creeping infallibility," to use the words of Charles Curran,[45] regarding the faithful's response to noninfallible but authoritative judgments. In the view of some revisionists, Grisez calls for greater respect and authority to be given to such judgments than is warranted by their status. Grisez writes, "When a faithful Catholic's best judgment is formed, as it should be, by the Church's noninfallible teaching, the Catholic might possibly be following a false norm. Yet God has provided no better norm for his or her current belief and practice."[46] To give such judgments this authority in cases where there are strong contrary arguments is to both deny the role and function of the primacy of conscience[47] and to ignore history. First, Christian tradition has consistently defended the authority of conscience in moral matters. Aquinas writes regarding the application of knowledge to action, "Conscience is said to bind by force of the divine precept."[48] That is, as long as one acts according to one's well-formed and informed conscience, even in the case of invincible ignorance and an erroneous judgment of conscience, that conscience maintains its dignity.[49] While it certainly is the case that one who informs one's conscience according to the noninfallible authoritative teachings of the magisterium is not morally culpable if this teaching is erroneous, it does not follow that, given serious reasons that conflict with the claims of those teachings, one who acts against them *is* morally culpable. Revisionists argue that while there is always a strong presumption of truth in favor of magisterial teaching, if there are serious reasons for questioning that teaching, one can indeed knowingly and willingly act against such a teaching on the authority of conscience. One only need look at the history of the church to see that, especially in questions of morals, the magisterium has erred on noninfallible judgments, even grievously.[50] Pope John Paul II's recent acknowledgement of the sins of the sons of the church attests to this fact.[51] If individual Christians err, including those acting in a magisterial capacity, it is proof not of the limits of the Holy Spirit but of the limits of human beings to respond faithfully to the Spirit. All human beings, including members of the magisterium, are subject to sin and its impact on the discernment of truth. And while the church as a whole cannot err in matters of belief,[52] discerning the implications of that belief for moral teaching is an ongoing process. The church has erred in moral matters in the past. However, the church as a pilgrim church in the process of becoming provides hope that error will not persist in the long term.

Fifth, revisionism would contrast the ecclesiology developed by the BGT and their reliance upon *Humani Generis* and *Lumen Gentium* 25 with that developed elsewhere in *Lumen Gentium* and other Vatican II documents. For example, *Gaudium et Spes* reflects a communion ecclesiology:

> With the help of the Holy Spirit, it is the task of the entire People of God, especially pastors and theologians, to hear, distinguish, and interpret the many voices of our age, and to judge them in the light of the divine Word. In this way, revealed truth can always be more deeply penetrated, better understood, and set forth to greater advantage.[53]

One might ask how such ecclesiological models at variance with one another could evolve from the same council? Not only does the hermeneutical lens determine one's interpretation of these documents, but also, as McCormick notes, "It is a known and acknowledged fact that the documents of Vatican II contain perspectives and statements that are ill at ease with each other."[54] In revisionism's ecclesiology, legitimate and respectful dissent is a part of the dialogical model between theologians and the magisterium. It is not a cancer to be eliminated but a service to the church in her ongoing journey to discern how we respond to complex moral questions through an ongoing reflection on revelation.

Finally, while the BGT would strictly limit those issues that are open to discussion between theologians and the magisterium, revisionism would maintain that all noninfallible magisterial pronouncements are open to scholarly investigation.

The revisionist dialogical model is based on the two components of dialogue itself, listening and speaking. For theologians, the listening pole entails several dimensions. First, as Catholic theologians, they must listen to the magisterium and its authoritative teaching as the Holy Spirit guides it. This is so because the magisterium is not just another source or authority for theologians. It is a *religious* authority. As such, it is to be trusted because Christ has promised that he will not abandon his church to error.[55] Those who are in positions of authority within the church have been promised the guidance of the Holy Spirit, and this fundamental truth does not allow the theologian to view the authority of the magisterium as an equal, much less a competing authority, among others. Second, theologians must listen to the Holy Spirit guiding them in their own spiritual journey. This journey includes all dimensions of their lives, including scholarship. There is a *scholarly pneumatology* within the theological discipline. (Indeed, I would see the call to be a theologian as a vocation, just as the call to be a priest, married, or celibate is a vocation. One is not limited to a single vocation in life.) Third, theologians must listen to their own scholarship and research, including all the sources of moral knowledge, and must try to discern the truth in community in light of that scholarship. In light of these three components, theologians must speak. Dissent is not the *purpose* of the listening process, but can certainly be a component of this process when there are serious reasons for questioning noninfallible magisterial teachings. Revisionist theologians, in fact, dissent on a very narrow range of ethical issues. Their dissent, however, has attracted a disproportionate amount of attention. In other words, the issues on which there is dissent are rather miniscule in comparison to the agreement between theologians and the magisterium. For its part, the magisterium, both bishops and pope, must engage in much of the same processes of listening, as do theologians. Granted that the magisterium is promised the guidance of the Holy Spirit, as are the faithful as a whole, the Holy Spirit can only do so much. The work of the Holy Spirit produces its effects through finite and sinful human beings, who, as history has shown, can fail to cooperate. Because of human finitude and sin, this cooperation is not always present, either for theologians or the magisterium. Given the profound role of the magisterium to teach authoritatively within the church, it has a greater burden, and thus a greater responsibility, in learning and searching out truth in light of "the signs of the times." Part of this learning and searching entails not only the magisterium's own listening in the form of discernment, research, scholarship, and prayer, but also dialoguing with theologians in order to aid the magisterium in this process. Thus, while maintaining a central position in the learning-teaching process, the magisterium cannot dispense with the process.

"Universal Consensus": Theologians and the Magisterium

The different ecclesiological models and models of the relationship between the magisterium and theologians lead to two fundamentally different hermeneutics of church documents on the criteria for determining whether or not a pronouncement of the ordinary universal magisterium is infallible, the second issue to be addressed between the BGT and revisionism. Similar to the investigation of scripture and its methodological function in ethical theory,[56] the selection of church documents, and their interpretation and application, both shape and reflect one's theory as well. While a detailed investigation of these texts would take us beyond the scope of this work, I will focus on a paragraph from *Lumen Gentium* used by both the BGT and revisionism. Based on different interpretations of this text, each theory derives very different conclusions on its implications for tradition as a source of moral knowledge.

Lumen Gentium 25 states the following with regard to the infallibility of the ordinary universal magisterium:

> Although the individual bishops do not enjoy the prerogative of infallibility, they can nevertheless proclaim Christ's doctrine infallibly. This is so, even when they are dispersed around the world, provided that while maintaining the bond of unity among themselves and with Peter's successor, and while teaching authentically on a matter of faith or morals, they concur in a single viewpoint as the one that must be held conclusively.[57]

Germain Grisez and Francis A. Sullivan have extensively debated the numerous conditions laid out for declaring a teaching of the ordinary universal magisterium infallible, especially with regard to the magisterium's teaching on artificial birth control.[58] A particularly contentious point of debate between these two scholars on this paragraph from *Lumen Gentium* concerns the criteria for determining whether or not a judgment has been proposed conclusively or definitively and is thus infallible. One way of determining whether or not this is the case is explained in the 1983 *Code of Canon Law,* namely, that such a teaching has been infallibly defined must be "clearly established." There must be "universal consensus" on this teaching.[59] What are the epistemological criteria for determining such a consensus? Whose "universal consensus" is required? Is it a universal consensus of bishops, theologians, the faithful, or solely a "firm and consistent" teaching of the papacy? How important is theological consensus in determining whether or not an infallible statement has been issued by the ordinary universal magisterium? Given the importance of such a statement, it would seem that there would be no doubt, especially among theologians *and* bishops, regarding the status of such a teaching. In his final point in one of their exchanges, Grisez asserts,

> *for theologians,* lack of consensus for a position is no argument against it, and an alleged consensus for a position is a bad argument in its favor....Methodologically...this at best

provides an unreliable sign of where the truth might lie. And logically, it provides no justification for participating in the alleged consensus; invoked as a response to a reasoned theological argument, it is fallacious.[60]

In his reply to Grisez on this particular exchange between the two, Sullivan deems it important enough to their overall dialogue to focus on "the significance of the fact that there is no evidence of a consensus among Catholic theologians" on the infallibility of the teaching by the ordinary universal magisterium prohibiting the use of artificial contraception.[61] Given this lack of consensus for the Ford-Grisez thesis on the infallible teaching on artificial birth control developed in an earlier article,[62] Sullivan maintains that "it can hardly be 'clearly established' that the official doctrine on artificial contraception has been infallibly taught...." Consequently, "it does not qualify as irreformable teaching."[63] The "consensus of Catholic theologians" is a basic consideration of Sullivan's response to Grisez for determining whether or not this (or, one may presume, any) doctrine has been infallibly taught by the ordinary universal magisterium. To support his argument, Sullivan cites Pius IX's letter *Tuas Libenter* and a more recent statement by the International Theological Commission, *On the Interpretation of Dogma.*[64] Whereas Grisez "belittles the importance of such a [theological] consensus,"[65] according to Sullivan, both of these documents highlight its importance. With regard to the former document, Sullivan concludes:

> Given the connection that Pius IX saw between the fact that a doctrine was being taught by the ordinary universal magisterium, and the presence of a constant and universal consensus among Catholic theologians upholding that same doctrine, it follows that in the absence of such a consensus among Catholic theologians, it would be difficult to maintain that a doctrine had been taught by the ordinary universal magisterium as definitively to be held. But this is precisely what Grisez wishes to maintain.[66]

While Grisez acknowledges, "Sullivan has drawn from *Tuas Libenter* a theological argument for the importance of the consensus of Catholic theologians," it is *authentic,* and not *alleged* consensus that fulfills its stipulations.[67] One might pose the following question to Grisez: What constitutes the difference between these two types of consensus? Why does the pre-1962 consensus of bishops and theologians that he and Ford cite in favor of the infallibility of the norm prohibiting the use of artificial birth control represent an authentic consensus,[68] and therefore a legitimate component to "help gauge the 'weight of this uniform teaching,'"[69] whereas any subsequent lack of consensus among *both* bishops and theologians[70] that challenges their conclusions is not an authentic *lack* of consensus that should also help in analyzing its authority? Grisez maintains that, given the state of theology today where "some contemporary theologians deny infallibility altogether, and quite a few deny that it can extend to specific moral norms," as well as the fact that "neither uninterrupted Christian tradition nor repeated and forceful papal reaffirmations of a traditional teaching impress those who deny it…the absence of theological consensus about the status of moral teachings no longer has the significance it would have had in 1863."[71] In addition, radical dissenting theologians have influenced bishops as well,[72] thereby lessening even the bishops' credibility in contributing to "authentic consensus."[73] Grisez attributes this state of the theological discipline, as well as what he regards a crisis in the church, to a radical dissent that gained a foothold at Vatican II and has spread like a cancer within the church. In order to correct these ills and establish "authentic consensus" among Catholic theologians, the BGT would establish a right relationship between the magisterium and theologians. This right relationship consists of the juridical model presented above.

What are we to say concerning this exchange between Grisez and Sullivan on "universal consensus" between theologians (and bishops) as a consideration for determining whether or not a doctrine has been infallibly taught by the ordinary universal magisterium? First, Grisez's statement that, methodologically, consensus or the lack thereof is an "unreliable sign of where the truth might lie" is true, but requires qualification. Lack of consensus is unreliable in that it may not indicate precisely where the truth might lie, but it can certainly indicate where the truth does not lie. Perhaps it is an indication that we need to search out truth elsewhere in light of the sources of moral knowledge in the historical, cultural context in which we live. Second, to my knowledge, and as Sullivan's own response to Grisez makes clear, no one uses the argument of consensus, *in se,* "as a response to a reasoned theological argument." That is, no theologian would, or has, responded to Grisez's argument that, in spite of your reasoned argument for artificial birth control as an infallible norm, the lack of consensus of theologians on the status of this teaching invalidates your argument. The lack of consensus is not merely a numbers game; it is reflective of the strengths or weaknesses of the arguments proposed behind consensus or lack thereof. Therefore, revisionism would agree with Grisez that consensus, in itself, proves nothing.

Third, and more to the point, Sullivan's and Grisez's exchange on the role and function of theological consensus as a consideration for determining whether or not the ordinary universal magisterium has issued an infallible statement seems to be given too much importance in their exchanges. It seems that this would be a crucial consideration for the question of infallible pronouncements by the ordinary universal magisterium *only if* universal theological consensus were a *necessary* condition for an infallible teaching, or somehow constitutive of it. While such consensus is certainly not essential for this determination, however, the *connection* between a lack of theological consensus and a teaching can be enlightening on two accounts. First, the arguments proposed by theologians that challenge a particular magisterial teaching *may,* through an ongoing dialogue between theologians and the magisterium, indicate that the teaching needs to be explored, refined, clarified, or in extreme cases, abandoned.

Second, the role and function of theological consensus in one's ethical method indicates how one perceives the relationship between theologians and the magisterium and indicates, more basically, the ecclesiology of a particular ethical method. As indicated above, the arguments and reflections proposed by many revisionist theologians based on the four sources of moral knowledge, which is at the heart of the lack of theological consensus on the teaching on artificial birth control, have not been adequately responded to by the papacy. Rather, the response has been an authoritative reaffirmation of a traditional teaching. It is clear that what is at the heart of the debate over theological consensus and infallible teachings by the ordinary universal magisterium is as much (if not more) about authority, its exercise, role, and function in the current papacy, as about the theological arguments for or against a particular ethical issue.

Grisez's identification of the lack of consensus amongst bishops with the influence of radically dissenting theologians that rules out authentic consensus, and his interpretation that radical dissent reflects a cancer in the church, represents a serious statement on *how* the Holy Spirit works within the church. One could reasonably assert that Grisez's position on authentic and alleged consensus is intimately tied to a very narrow, papal ecclesiology. That is, it is not the college of bishops who are God's voice on earth, but only those bishops who conform to papal statements unconditionally. Such an ecclesiology virtually rules out authentic pluralism within the church. Not only do Grisez and Sullivan differ on the criteria for establishing "universal consensus," but the BGT and revisionism also disagree fundamentally on the proper object of the ordinary universal magisterium's infallible teachings.

Ethical Method and tradition:
The Secondary Object of Infallibility?

Both the BGT and revisionism agree that if a natural law norm is also contained in divine revelation, then that norm falls under the auspices of the primary object of infallibility. They further agree that any infallible teaching of the magisterium belonging to the primary object of infallibility requires an assent of "divine and Catholic faith." A point of contention concerns those norms that belong to the secondary object of infallibility, i.e., truths not contained in divine revelation, but which are required for revelation's explanation and defense. The BGT maintains that the ordinary magisterium has taught infallibly such specific natural law norms; revisionism denies this claim. In this section, I will present two fundamental differences between the theories that draw from tradition yet support contradictory positions on this issue: First, the distinction between two types of moral truths; second, the distinction between the first principles of the natural law and the secondary precepts that are derived from them.

A fundamental question that divides revisionism and the BGT is whether or not specific natural law norms have been, or even can be, taught infallibly by the ordinary universal magisterium. In other words, are such norms (e.g., forbidding contraception) necessary to safeguard and defend the deposit of faith or revelation? The question is about the appropriate *object* of such infallible teachings. According to the BGT, the teaching prohibiting artificial birth control, for example, "is at least connected with [revelation] as a truth required to guard the deposit as inviolable and to expound it with fidelity."[74] In this sense, the norm forbidding artificial birth control and similar norms are "truths of salvation," i.e., they are moral truths in which the charism of the magisterium, through the guidance of the Holy Spirit, is equipped to teach infallibly. Josef Fuchs, S.J., responds to moral theologians (among them could be included Grisez and Ford) who have attempted to argue that such norms are "truths of salvation"; in so doing, he distinguishes between two types of moral truths.[75] According to Fuchs, moral truths can be divided into those that relate to moral goodness and moral rightness; these two categories of moral truths distinguish the magisterium's teaching charism and competence. Moral goodness pertains to the person as such and his or her character, motive, disposition, etc. Fundamentally, it asks whether or not the person is open and committed to God's self-giving love. It is the vertical dimension of the person that relates to the person's salvation. Moral goodness, however, is always realized in the world of other persons. This is the horizontal dimension of the person and is designated by moral rightness. Moral rightness is concerned with the kind of activity that facilitates human well-being. Strictly speaking, the adjective *moral* pertains to goodness alone. It is used with *rightness* only in an analogous sense. That is, "'Moral' in its proper and formal sense refers only to persons and their free attitudes and decisions, but, because personal moral goodness contains concern for the well-being of the human world as its moral task, it urges 'right' activity within this world; and only because of this relationship between personal goodness and material rightness, this rightness is also called moral rightness."[76] Truths of salvation pertain to moral goodness whereas material norms indicate right or wrong behavior. According to Fuchs and other revisionist moral theologians,[77] only the former can be considered as the proper object of the secondary object of infallibility and are within the competence of the magisterium to teach.

To defend this assertion, Fuchs has recourse to scripture, tradition, and magisterial documents. The upshot of his argument is threefold. First, these sources reveal that, whereas the magisterium has taught infallibly on questions of natural law that are revealed, it has not taught infallibly on nonrevealed questions of natural law (e.g., contraception). Second, there is agreement among theologians that the competence of the magisterium to guide the church community is promised by the Holy Spirit. There is disagreement, however, that this competence extends to questions of rightness/wrongness and material norms. McCormick, for example, demonstrates how, in comparison to pre-Vatican II magisterial teachings, the documents of Vatican II and subsequent magisterial teachings have clearly limited the claims of the magisterium's competence to judge in the area of rightness/wrongness.[78] Finally, Fuchs and other revisionists would classify norms such as those prohibiting contraception, masturbation, reproductive technologies, etc., as moral truths that pertain to material norms of rightness and wrongness, not truths of salvation that pertain to moral goodness. As such, they cannot be considered as the proper object of infallible teaching.

One of the texts that Fuchs and many other revisionists cite to justify their argument against the plausibility of teaching non-revealed infallible natural law norms is *Gaudium et Spes* 33: "The Church guards the heritage of God's Word and draws from it religious and moral principles, *without always having at hand the solution to particular problems.*"[79] Religious and moral principles relate to truths of salvation and moral goodness, whereas solutions to particular problems relate to material norms and rightness/wrongness. The BGT gives two responses to revisionism's use of this and similar texts to argue its position. In his response to revisionists who make "some play" with this and similar texts to deny absolute norms that belong to the secondary object of infallibility, John Finnis asserts that revisionists have committed a non sequitur by overlooking the distinction between "not every" and "not any." In doing so, they move from "'The church cannot give a specific answer to *every* moral question' to 'The church cannot teach with definitive authority *any* specific moral norm.'"[80] In his references, he cites Sullivan, Fuchs, and Gerard Hughes, S.J., as theologians who have repeatedly committed this non sequitur. According to Finnis, then, revisionists have taken great liberty in their hermeneutic of passages from Vatican II to deny that some norms, especially those that belong to the secondary object of infallibility, have been taught infallibly by the magisterium.

Grisez has another response to revisionism. In his response, he cites a passage from *Gaudium et Spes* that substantiates that there are some specific moral norms whose truth precludes substantial revision: "Contemplating this melancholy state of humanity, the Council wishes to recall first of all the permanent binding force of universal natural law and its all-embracing principles.

Man's conscience itself gives ever more emphatic voice to these principles."[81]

In response to Grisez's point, revisionism has recourse to Aquinas's *Summa Theologiae*. Richard McCormick and John Mahoney note that Aquinas distinguishes between the first principles of natural law and secondary precepts or certain detailed proximate conclusions that flow from those principles.[82] Whereas the first principles of natural law cannot change and are, therefore, absolute, the characteristics of the secondary precepts or application of the first principles are, in the words of McCormick, "provisionality, flexibility and contingency."[83] In contemporary theological terminology, we could say that these secondary precepts are material norms that relate to rightness and wrongness and are subject to change, clarification, and evolution in light of their ongoing dialogue with the signs of the times (e.g., history, culture, and tradition).

The BGT recognizes Aquinas's distinction between principles and their application as well. It further recognizes that revisionism cites this article from Aquinas "to support their view that one must decide in each case whether a received moral norm must be fulfilled or is overridden by other considerations."[84] In response to revisionism's use of Aquinas, Grisez notes the following: First, while it may be the case that Aquinas's statement may be true "with respect to most specific norms," he does teach "that there are norms that do not admit of exception."[85] Second, he posits that Aquinas's assertion, drawn from Aristotle's physics distinguishing between what is universal and absolute versus what is contingent and changing, is fallacious. It is based on a misperception of the existential, moral domain and the natural world.

> The whole morally significant content of one's action must be intelligible, since one is responsible only for what one understands. For this reason, proposals one adopts by choice never are morally particularized by unique, unrepeatable, material, contingent factors. *The really unique*

aspects of one's action make no difference whatsoever to the morality of what one does.[86]

Finnis also acknowledges revisionism's use of this passage from Aquinas. He asserts that revisionism makes "much play" with this statement to show "that derived moral norms, since they involve contingent particulars, hold not universally but only generally (ut in pluribus), subject to exceptions (*ut in paucioribus*)."[87] Finnis points out, however, that while many positive norms admit of exceptions, there are negative absolute norms that apply "always and everywhere without exceptions."[88]

What can be said of this seemingly interminable debate between revisionism and the BGT and their conflicting interpretation of tradition as to whether or not the ordinary magisterium has taught infallibly specific natural law norms that belong to the secondary object of infallibility? There are at least three methodological differences that shape each school's hermeneutical lens for interpreting tradition. The first entails what each school considers to be the moral realm. In their responses to revisionists, neither Grisez nor Finnis (who specifically cites Fuchs's article, which we discussed earlier) consider the distinction of moral truths, i.e., goodness and truths of salvation or rightness and the fulfillment of human well-being. The distinction between these terms and the norms that correspond to each reflect a more foundational view of the moral realm itself.

Many revisionists evaluate the rightness or wrongness of an act in terms of the human person adequately considered and how the act impacts its dimensions, aside from the subjective motivation or moral goodness of the agent choosing the act.[89] The relationship between the act and its impact on those dimensions defines objective morality for revisionism. So, for example, whereas giving alms for the sake of vainglory is morally blameworthy (bad), what of the impact of that act on the poor? Revisionism would say that the act is right, but the motive and act defined in terms of the motive is morally bad. The BGT, however, does not view the moral realm in these terms. For the BGT, "moral acts are *objectively* constituted by what people think they are doing. Subjective morality is in the possibility of a person's confusion and/or error about the moral or badness of his or her act, and in the possibility that a person's freedom to choose is blocked or impeded."[90] In the case of almsgiving, then, the BGT would say that the act is morally bad since the agent thinks that he is doing the act to gain praise rather than to relieve the suffering of the poor. The BGT does not have the ethical tools to evaluate the impact of the act, *in se,* on human well-being detached from the subjective goodness/badness of the moral agent. So, for example, regardless of whether or not a person *actually* performs an act, intention itself is morally decisive in the BGT's understanding of objective morality. A person who thinks about murdering another person is a murderer, regardless of whether or not he commits the act of murder.[91] Objective morality, then, resides within the willing subject, regardless of the impact of carrying out one's intentions in actions and their impact on human well-being. The BGT, however, is not entirely consistent in its claim. For instance, if a couple *thinks* that they are practicing responsible parenthood by using artificial birth control, why would this not determine the objective morality of their act? While the BGT posits a moral order where there is an intrinsic relationship between certain acts (e.g., artificial birth control) and the will choosing the act (a contraceptive will), revisionism would deny this moral order and, consequently, this intrinsic relationship. It is on the basis of this moral order that the BGT posits specific natural law norms that belong to the secondary object of infallibility that have been taught by the ordinary universal magisterium. Though Grisez and Boyle claim that they are confident that their position on the objective/subjective distinction, as well as other distinctions, "consistently develop[s] Catholic tradition,"[92] their assertion is certainly debatable.[93]

The second methodological difference is in how each theory defines and classifies a norm. Determining whether or not a specific natural law norm has been taught infallibly by the ordinary universal magisterium depends, in large part, on this definition.[94]

Many revisionists recognize three types of moral norms—material, formal, and synthetic. Material norms are premoral, nonabsolute norms that indicate certain premoral disvalues (or values) that tend to have a negative (or positive) impact on human wellbeing, and pertain to rightness and wrongness. Formal norms are moral, absolute norms that indicate a morally good or bad character, motive, or disposition and pertain to moral goodness (i.e., truths of salvation) or badness. Synthetic norms are moral absolutes that describe an act (killing), the motive (malevolence), and circumstances (unjustified) such as do not murder.

The BGT recognizes revisionism's distinction between various types of norms (material and formal), but proposes another type of specific moral norm. "The description of the act goes beyond mere behavior [material norm], yet does not go so far as to build in the moral determinant [formal or synthetic norm]." Such norms can be absolute norms if they are "formulated with respect to the moral act, which includes the wrongful choice."[95] Therefore, any choice of an act prohibited by the norm would necessarily be morally bad. Since a specific norm entails a presumption about the nature of the will that chooses an act proscribed by the norm, there can be absolute specific natural law norms. Such norms would be the proper object for the magisterium's teaching on the primary (part of revelation) or secondary (truths closely associated with revelation) object of infallibility. Revisionists, however, refer to such norms as synthetic norms. For example, whereas murder and lying are always morally bad, killing and falsehoods are not always such, precisely because the former include a description of a disordered will whereas the latter do not.

For revisionism, the possibility of evolution, change, and development—in a word, historical consciousness—within the human experience rules out, by definition, material natural law norms that could be taught infallibly by the magisterium. A necessary prerequisite for infallibility is that a teaching is irreformable, that is, "the formulation [of an infallible teaching] can be improved, but the meaning must be retained."[96] According to Sullivan, however, "We can never exclude the possibility that future experience, hitherto unimagined, might put a moral problem into a new frame of reference which would call for a revision of a norm that, when formulated, could not have taken such new experience into account."[97] In response, Grisez cites genocide as a specific moral norm that is an absolute and, therefore, could be considered the subject of an infallible judgment by the magisterium.[98] No future experience could put genocide into a new frame of reference that would transform the norm prohibiting genocide from an absolute to a non-absolute norm. As noted above, however, the point of contention here would not be on whether or not genocide is an absolute norm, but on the *nature* of the norm being debated. Revisionism denies the existence of absolute material norms, not absolute synthetic norms that include both a description of the act and the moral nature of the will choosing the act. Genocide, like murder, by definition contains its very moral condemnation in the term itself. Both schools would agree that the norm prohibiting genocide is a moral absolute, yet they would disagree on the appropriate act-descriptions in other specific moral norms.

In Grisez's quotation cited above on Aquinas's use of Aristotle, there is some ambiguity in how we are to interpret Grisez's final sentence. What does Grisez mean when he writes: "The really unique aspects of one's action make no difference whatsoever to the morality of what one does"? This question reveals the third methodological distinction between the BGT and revisionism. While both schools agree that certain actions are always wrong (e.g., murder, theft, or adultery), they disagree fundamentally on the morally relevant circumstances that can determine whether or not an individual situation corresponds to the act defined and prohibited by a norm.[99] Much of this debate centers on the definition of the object and the traditional sources of morality.[100] Why is it that the unique aspect that a person is becoming intoxicated in lieu of an anesthetic in preparation for a painful operation is morally significant to the description of the act and the application of the norm prohibiting the act ("one should not drink oneself into a stupor")[101] whereas the fact that a married couple is using a condom to prevent the spread of an STD is not an aspect that justifies redefining the act and the norm prohibiting that act?[102] Is that not precisely what Aquinas means in asserting that, while general principles hold, their specific application varies according to the unique context or circumstances? Certainly revisionism would agree that unique aspects make no difference to morality *if* those aspects are not morally significant. However, Grisez does not provide a clear definition for what he considers to be the "unique aspects of one's actions" or criteria for determining whether or not they affect the morality of what one does. For if it is the case that "one's morally significant act will include only what one deliberately chooses to do and permit—that is, what one understands about what one is doing—and one's practical understanding can be wholly determined by moral principles,"[103] what purpose do specific norms play? In addition, does not this open the door to rampant subjectivism that the BGT clearly rejects? For the BGT, it seems that dispensing from some (but not all) of the "unique aspects of one's action" is essential to posit certain specific norms as absolutes and, therefore, as the appropriate object of the secondary object of infallibility taught by the ordinary magisterium.

From the foregoing, it is clear not only that the BGT and revisionism have very unique understandings of Tradition and tradition as sources of moral knowledge that shape their ethical theories, but also that the other sources of moral knowledge and the hermeneutic of those sources impact their perception of Tradition and tradition as well. Methodology is a dialectical process of creating a synthetic whole out of the various sources of moral knowledge. As a theological ethic, the BGT has a clear hierarchy of the sources of moral knowledge. Tradition, specifically the magisterium as the teaching authority in the Church on faith and morals, is at the pinnacle of this hierarchy and functions as a hermeneutical lens for its interpretation of revelation. Its deontological normative methodology justifies, philosophically, its claim to absolute norms. While revisionism recognizes the magisterium as a preeminent methodological source of moral knowledge, it insists that the magisterium must be evaluated in its moral teaching capacity in light of all the other sources of moral knowledge. The theological justification for its perspective lies in Tradition and the fundamental shift in ecclesiology at Vatican II from a hierarchical model to a communion model. Philosophically, experience and reason, as these have been developed into the mixed teleological principle of proportionate reason, are central to determining right or wrong acts and resolving conflicts when two or more material norms conflict.

Conclusion

Germain Grisez and Joseph Boyle note the following in a recent exchange between themselves and Edward Vacek, a representative of proportionalism or revisionism.

> In our view, the great merit of Vacek's contribution is that, though narrowly focused on one argument about one kind of moral act [artificial birth control], it exhibits very clearly the nature and extent of the disagreement between proportionalists and us. As Grisez's mentor, Richard McKeon, powerfully demonstrated, sound interpretations of philosophical opponents' positions often are impeded—and attempts to criticize their seemingly obvious errors often are vitiated— by the theoretical gulf between views that radically differ in their principles and methods.[104]

There are two important points to note in this statement. The first concerns the conceptual and terminological ambiguities that make dialogue difficult between the two theories. For example, the definition of moral and premoral, specific norms and material, formal, or synthetic norms, objective and subjective, the human act, etc., all impede an understanding of the opposing ethical theory and, thus, productive and constructive dialogue between them. In a word, the two methods themselves are incommensurable. The second point, however, is that in addition to the conceptual ambiguities, the two schools have fundamentally different views of the sources of moral knowledge, their hermeneutic, priority, and interrelationship. This work has extensively investigated those methodological considerations that divide the two theories fundamentally. A basic question for Catholic ethical method is, in light of those divisions, Is there any possibility of reaching common ground between the two theories?

The most promising area of discourse, and one which we often lose sight of in academic exchanges, is that both theories attempt more adequately to articulate our shared Christian heritage as this pertains to concrete praxis. Both theories recognize the impact of Christianity on the individual and communal perception of reality and the acts that follow from, and shape, that perception. Furthermore, both recognize that our acts, over time, shape who we are and who we are striving to become as believing Christians. Even in this basic insight, however, the ethical perspective that develops out of it differs between the two theories fundamentally. The BGT posits this insight in terms of one's vocation to live out a life of Christian charity in and through faith. Revisionism posits it in terms of moving toward, or returning to, an ethics of virtue that is both nourished by faith and grace, and guides our actions and choices that we make as human beings. It seems to me that some promising work could be done in describing vocation and virtue in terms that are acceptable to both schools of thought. This is especially the case, given the emphasis on virtue in the life of the Christian throughout tradition. The reunification of spirituality and moral theology, divided after the Council of Trent, seems promising in terms of both vocation and virtue. Working out this common ground is a possibility for future work in Catholic normative ethical method.[105]

Notes

Introduction

1. The theologians who represent this school are too numerous to list here. However, invaluable sources that cite both those theologians and their contributions to the revisionist school of thought are the ongoing "Notes on Moral Theology," published annually in *Theological Studies,* and the series, *Readings in Moral Theology* (New York/Mahwah, NJ: Paulist Press), edited by Charles E. Curran, Richard A. McCormick, S.J., and Margaret A. Farley (volume nine).

2. Pope John Paul II, *Veritatis Splendor* (Vatican City: Libreria Editrice Vaticana, 1993).

3. *Veritatis Splendor,* par. 75.

4. Ibid., pars. 13, 48, 50, 67, 79. See Grisez, *Difficult Moral Questions: The Way of the Lord Jesus, Volume Three* (Quincy IL: Franciscan Press, 1997) [hereinafter, *DMQ*] 851, n. 440; Grisez and Joseph Boyle, "Response to Our Critics and Collaborators," in Robert P. George, ed., *Natural Law and Moral Inquiry: Ethics, Metaphysics, and Politics in the Work of Germain Grisez* (Washington, DC: Georgetown University Press, 1998), 221–22; William E. May, "Germain Grisez on Moral Principles and Moral Norms: Natural and Christian," in ibid., 23–25; Charles E. Curran, *The Catholic Moral Tradition Today: A Synthesis* (Washington, DC: Georgetown University Press, 1999), 159; Jean Porter, "'Direct' and 'Indirect' in Grisez's Moral Theory," *Theological*

Studies 57 (1996), 611; and Joseph A. Selling, "Ideological Differences: Some Background Considerations for Understanding *Veritatis Splendor,*" *The Month* 24 (January 1994), 12–14.

    5. For anthologies discussing the encyclical and its misrepresentation of the revisionist position, see Joe Selling and Jan Jans, eds., *The Splendor of Accuracy: An Examination of the Assertions made by Veritatis Splendor* (Kampen, Netherlands: Kok Pharos Publishing House, 1994); Michael E. Allsopp and John J. O'Keefe, eds., *Veritatis Splendor: American Responses* (Kansas City, MO: Sheed & Ward, 1995); and John Wilkins, ed., *Considering Veritatis Splendor* (Cleveland, Ohio: Pilgrim Press, 1994).

    6. See, for example, Thomas Aquinas, *S.T.,* I, q. 1, a. 5.

    7. I am using the term *Catholic normative ethical method* or its variants (e.g., Catholic ethical method) to designate those dimensions that have emerged out of the Catholic Christian tradition that this tradition shares with Christian normative ethical method (e.g., Christology) but which is also specific to the Catholic tradition (e.g., the magisterium).

    8. See Bernard Häring, *The Law of Christ: Moral Theology for Priests and Laity,* 3 vols., E.G. Kaiser, trans. (Westminster, MD: Newman Press, 1963).

    9. *Optatam Totius,* in Walter M. Abbott, ed., *The Documents of Vatican II* (New York: America Press, 1966) [hereinafter, *Documents*], par. 16, 452.

    10. For an explanation of these terms, see below.

    11. Henry J. McCloskey, *Meta-ethics and Normative Ethics* (The Hague: Martinus Nijhoff, 1969), 7; and John D. Arras, Bonnie Steinbock, and Alex John London, "Moral Reasoning in the Medical Context," in Arras and Steinbock (eds.), *Ethical Issues in Modern Medicine* (London: Mayfield Publishing Co., 1999, 5th ed.), 1–40.

    12. *Gaudium et Spes,* in *Documents,* par. 51, 256. It may be somewhat problematic to impose the philosophical rightness/goodness distinction on Vatican documents. However, Catholic tradition has long recognized the distinction between the objective and subjective dimensions of human activity, though it has not always consistently adhered to this distinction. Philosophical ethics helps to ground this distinction.

    13. Todd A. Salzman, "The Human Act and Its Moral Evaluation in the *Catechism of the Catholic Church:* A Critical Analysis," in

Michael E. Allsopp, ed., *Ethics and the Catechism of the Catholic Church* (Scranton: University of Scranton Press, 1999), 68–71.

14. William K. Frankena, *Ethics* (Englewood Cliffs, NJ: Prentice Hall, 2nd ed., 1973), 96.

15. Gilbert Harman, *The Nature of Morality: An Introduction to Ethics* (New York: Oxford University Press, 1977), 11.

16. See Grisez, *The Way of the Lord Jesus, Volume One: Christian Moral Principles* (Chicago: Franciscan Herald Press, 1983) [hereinafter, *CMP*], 102–3.

17. Frankena, *Ethics,* 96.

18. See Aquinas, *S.T.,* I–II, q. 91, a. 2; and q. 93.

19. Ibid., q. 94, a. 4; q. 91, a. 3, ad 3.

20. Ibid., q. 108, a. 2, ad 1: "Matters of faith are above human reason, and so we cannot attain to them except through grace. Consequently, when grace came to be bestowed more abundantly, the result was an increase in the number of explicit points of faith. On the other hand, it is through human reason that we are directed to works of virtue, for it is the rule of human action, as stated above. Wherefore in such matters as these there was no need for any precepts to be given besides the moral precepts of the Law, which proceed from the dictate of reason."

21. Whereas BGT emphasizes the distinction between natural law and divine law, especially as concerns specific norms, revisionism emphasizes the agreement between the two. See Grisez, *CMP,* 175–78.

22. See Josef Fuchs, S.J., *Natural Law: A Theological Investigation,* Helmut Reckter, S.J., trans. (New York: Sheed and Ward, 1965), 144–62.

23. Timothy O'Connell, *Principles for a Catholic Morality* (San Francisco: HarperSanFrancisco, 1990, rev. ed.), 205.

24. Abraham Edel, *Method in Ethical Theory* (New Brunswick, NJ: Transaction Publishers, 1994, new ed.), 4.

25. Curran, *The Catholic Moral Tradition Today,* 48.

26. *Gaudium et Spes,* in *Documents,* par. 44, 246.

27. Curran, *The Catholic Moral Tradition Today,* 54.

28. See *Dei Verbum,* in *Documents,* ch. 3, "The Divine Inspiration and the Interpretation of Scripture."

29. Pontifical Biblical Commission, "The Interpretation of the Bible in the Church," *Origins* 23/29 (January 6, 1994). For a presentation and analysis of other Biblical hermeneutical methods and theories,

see William C. Spohn, "Jesus and Christian Ethics: Notes on Moral Theology 1994," *Theological Studies* 56 (1995), 93–96.

30.   See P. C. Rodger and L. Vischer, eds., *The Fourth World Conference on Faith and Order: Montreal, 1963, Faith and Order Papers, No. 42* (London: SCM, 1964), nn. 38–63, 66–106. It should be noted that the distinction made in this document differs fundamentally from that posited within Catholic theological discourse. In that discourse, Tradition refers not simply to the process and structure but also to the content, whereas traditions refer to particular determinations of the Tradition, which may be permanent in certain contexts, but are not necessarily enduringly normative. (See Yves Congar, *Tradition and Traditions,* Michael Naseby and Thomas Rainborough, trans. [New York: The Macmillan Company, 1967].) Even within this discourse, however, there is fluidity in interpreting these two terms. For instance, while the International Theological Commission published a document entitled "The Interpretation of Dogmas," and uses the terms *Tradition* and *tradition* throughout the text, it provides no explanation of the terms (see "De interpretatione dogmatum," *Gregorianum* 72 [1991], 5–37).

31.   Curran, *The Catholic Moral Tradition Today,* 53.

32.   As we shall see, however, the early attempts of revisionism are more accurately described as developing an ethical norm or criterion to judge acts right or wrong rather than a normative method justifying norms of behavior.

33.   See Norbert Rigali, S.J., "On Christian Ethics," *Chicago Studies* 10 (1971), 227–47.

34.   See Spohn, *What Are They Saying about Scripture and Ethics?* (New York: Paulist Press, rev. ed., 1995), ch. 5.

35.   Curran, *The Catholic Moral Tradition Today,* 55.

36.   Germain Grisez, *CMP,* 10–11.

37.   See ibid., 7–11.

38.   Ibid.

1. Natural Law

1.   While *proportionalism* is the common term used to designate those moral theologians who utilize proportionate reason to determine right or wrong acts, the origins of revisionism precede Peter Knauer's

1965 article on the principle of double effect (see, for example, Bernard Häring, *Das Gesetz Christi: Moral theologie, dargestellt für Priester und Laien* [Freiburg I. Br.: Erich Wewel, 1954]) and includes broader methodological concerns. Consequently, in our discussion of Peter Knauer, we will use the term *proportionalism* to designate the school of thought that he influenced, recognizing that revisionism entails a wider methodological consideration than norms and normative ethics.

2. In magisterial documents, this discussion frequently revolves around how one defines the object of the act. Are certain acts intrinsically evil *ex objecto*, i.e., on the basis of the object alone without consideration of the circumstances or intention? Object, end or intention, and circumstances are known traditionally as the *fontes moralitatis* (sources of morality) and are the sources for determining the morality of an act. Given the complexity of defining the object, both revisionism and the BGT have questioned the usefulness of these terms. See Richard McCormick, S.J., *Notes on Moral Theology: 1981 through 1984* (Lanham, MD: University Press of America, 1984), 66; and Germain Grisez, *The Way of the Lord Jesus, Volume One: Christian Moral Principles* (Chicago: Franciscan Herald Press, 1983) [hereinafter, CMP, 247, n.3].

3. Grisez, *CMP,* 13–14.

4. Ibid., 14.

5. Some have questioned whether or not the Grisez-Finnis new natural law theory departs significantly from the older natural law. See, for example, Russell Hittinger, *A Critique of the New Natural Law Theory* (Notre Dame, IN: University of Notre Dame Press, 1987). For Grisez's response, see "A Critique of Russell Hittinger's Book, *A Critique of the New Natural Law Theory,*" *New Scholasticism* 62 (1988), 62–74.

6. Aquinas, *S.T.,* I–II, q. 19, a. 4 (see also, q. 91, a. 2; q. 94, a. 2; II–II, q. 47, a. 6). See Grisez, *CMP,* 173–75.

7. Aquinas, *S.T.,* I–II, q. 94, a. 2. See Grisez, *CMP,* 178–79.

8. D. J. O'Connor, *Aquinas and Natural Law* (London: Macmillan, 1967), 73. See John Finnis, *Natural Law and Natural Rights* (Oxford: Clarendon Press, 1980), 34.

9. David Hume, *A Treatise of Human Nature,* L.A. Selby-Bigge, ed. (Oxford: Oxford University Press, 1888), 469.

10. Germain Grisez and Russell Shaw, *Fulfillment in Christ: A Summary of Christian Moral Principles* (Notre Dame, IN: University of Notre Dame Press, 1991), 46.

11. Grisez, *CMP,* 105–6.

12. See Grisez, *CMP,* ch. 5.

13. The sources for the new natural law are extensive. Among them are the following: Grisez, *CMP; The Way of the Lord Jesus, Volume Two: Living a Christian Life* (Quincy, IL: Franciscan Herald Press, 1993) [hereinafter, *LCL*]; Grisez and Shaw, *Fulfillment in Christ;* John Finnis, *Natural Law and Natural Rights;* Finnis, *Fundamentals of Ethics* (Washington, DC: Georgetown University Press, 1983); Finnis, *Moral Absolutes: Tradition, Revision, and Truth* (Washington, DC: The Catholic University Press of America, 1991); Grisez, Joseph M. Boyle, and Finnis, *Nuclear Deterrence, Morality and Realism* (Oxford: Clarendon Press, 1987); and, id., "Practical Principles, Moral Truth and Ultimate Ends," *American Journal of Jurisprudence* 32 (1987), 99–151. For a synthesis of the BGT, see Jean Porter's "Basic Goods and the Human Good in Recent Catholic Moral Theology," *Thomist* 57 (1993), 28–42; and, "The Natural Law and the Specificity of Christian Morality: A Survey of Recent Work and an Agenda for Future Research," in Todd Salzman, ed., *Method and Catholic Moral Theology* (Omaha, NE: Creighton University Press, 1999), 209–29.

14. Grisez, *CMP,* 180 (emphasis deleted).

15. See Finnis, *Natural Law and Natural Rights,* 33–42.

16. Grisez and Shaw, *Fulfillment in Christ,* 77.

17. Ibid., 54.

18. John Finnis, *Natural Law and Natural Rights,* 34.

19. *CMP,* 124. See also Grisez, Boyle, and Finnis, "Practical Principles, Moral Truth and Ultimate Ends," 107–8.

20. Grisez, *Difficult Moral Questions: The Way of the Lord Jesus, Volume Three* (Quincy, IL: Franciscan Press, 1997), 854.

21. Whether or not the basic goods are moral or premoral goods is a fundamental point of contention between the BGT and revisionism. According to the BGT, they are premoral, not moral goods. In the BGT itself, however, there is an equivocation of the term *moral.* For example, Finnis states that the basic goods are not moral goods ("A Consistent Ethic—A Philosophical Critique," in Thomas G. Fuechtmann, ed., *Consistent Ethic of Life,* 176, n. 33). However, Grisez refers to the reflexive goods as "existential" or "moral" goods (*CMP,* 124). Given the absoluteness and inviolability of these goods, revisionism posits that they function as moral goods in the BGT (see, for example, James J. Walter, "Response to John C. Finnis: A Theological Critique," in *Consistent*

Ethic of Life, 186–87). Philosophers as well are critical of the lack of a clear distinction between moral and premoral in the BGT (see Ralph McInerny, "The Principles of Natural Law," in Curran and McCormick, S.J., eds., *Readings in Moral Theology No. 7: Natural Law and Theology* [New York: Paulist, 1991], 148–49; and Hittinger, *A Critique of the New Natural Law Theory,* 34–39).

22. Grisez and Shaw, *Fulfillment in Christ,* 80 (emphasis deleted).

23. Grisez, Boyle, and Finnis, "Practical Principles, Moral Truth and Ultimate Ends," 128.

24. Grisez and Shaw, *Fulfillment in Christ,* 86.

25. Grisez, *CMP,* 186.

26. Ibid. (emphasis deleted).

27. Ibid., 189 (emphasis deleted).

28. Ibid., 191 (emphasis deleted).

29. Ibid., 205–16 (emphasis deleted).

30. Ibid., 254.

31. Ibid., 255.

32. Ibid., ix (emphasis deleted).

33. See ibid., 233–34.

34. See for example Grisez and Boyle, "Response to Our Critics and Our Collaborators," in Robert P. George, ed., *Natural Law and Moral Inquiry: Ethics, Metaphysics, and Politics in the Work of Germain Grisez* (Washington, DC: Georgetown University Press, 1998), 219–22.

35. See Grisez, *LCL,* 266–68.

36. Grisez, *CMP,* 256–59.

37. Ibid.

38. See ibid., ch. 19; and William E. May, "Germain Grisez on Moral Principles and Moral Norms: Natural and Christian," in Robert P. George, ed., *Natural Law and Moral Inquiry,* 17–26.

39. Grisez, *CMP,* ch. 26.

40. Grisez, Boyle, and Finnis, *Nuclear Deterrence, Morality and Realism,* 278.

41. See William C. Spohn, "Jesus and Christian Ethics: Notes on Moral Theology 1994," *Theological Studies* 56 (1995), 101–7.

42. Jean Porter, *The Recovery of Virtue: The Relevance of Aquinas for Christian Ethics* (Louisville, KY: John Knox Press, 1990), 19–20.

43. Peter Knauer, "La détermination du bien et du mal moral par le principle du double effect," *Nouvelle revue theologique* 87 (1965) [hereinafter, cited as "La détermination"], 356–76, ([supplemented] English translation: "The Principle of Double Effect," *Theology Digest* 15 [1967], 100–104); for a reworking of the original French article, see "The Hermeneutic Function of the Principle of Double Effect," in Curran and McCormick, eds., *Readings in Moral Theology No. 1: Moral Norms and Catholic Tradition* (New York: Paulist Press, 1979), 1–39 [hereafter, cited as "The Hermeneutic Function"]. This version incorporates corrections and clarifications leveled against the original French article. Consequently, in my presentation of Knauer's position, I will have recourse to all three articles.

44. Grisez, *Abortion: The Myths, the Realities, the Arguments* (New York: Corpus, 1966), 331.

45. Knauer, "The Hermeneutic Function" 2; and, id., "Das rechtverstandene Prinzip von der Doppelwirkung als Grundnorm jeder Gewissensentsheidung," *Theologie und Glaube* 57 (1967), 107–33.

46. Ibid., 3.

47. Ibid., 1.

48. Knauer, "A Good End Does Not Justify an Evil Means— Even in Teleological Ethics," in Joseph A. Selling ed., *Personalist Morals: Essays in Honor of Professor Louis Janssens* (Leuven: Peeters Press, 1988), 77.

49. McCormick, *How Brave a New World?: Dilemmas in Bioethics* (Washington, DC: Georgetown University Press, 1981), 415.

50. Knauer, "La détermination," 357.

51. Bernard Hoose points out, however, that there is confusion in Knauer's position on the role of the direct/indirect distinction in the principle of double effect (see *Proportionalism,* 101–6).

52. Grisez, *CMP,* 154.

53. Finnis, *Moral Absolutes,* 14.

54. Walter, "The Foundation and Formulation of Norms, " in Charles E. Curran, ed., *Moral Theology: Challenges for the Future* (Mahwah, NJ: Paulist Press, 1990), 129.

55. Hoose, *Proportionalism,* 95.

56. Grisez, *CMP,* 160.

57. See the discussion of various realms of ethical discourse in the Introduction.

58. Hallett, *Greater Good: The Case for Proportionalism* (Washington, DC: Georgetown University Press, 1995), 4.

59. Ibid. 2–5.

60. Walter, "The Foundation and Formulation of Norms," 132.

61. See Hoose, *Proportionalism,* ch. 3.

62. Hoose, *Proportionalism,* 89.

63. Walter, "The Foundation and Formulation of Norms," 142.

64. Ibid., 129. See also Louis Janssens, "Ontic Good and Evil—Premoral Values and Disvalues," *Louvain Studies* 12 (1987), 81.

65. Formal, as it is used in relation to proportionate reason, means 'contentless,' and pertains to the rightness or wrongness of acts, not to the subjective goodness or badness of the moral agent, motive, etc.

66. Aquinas, following Cicero, lists seven relevant circumstances attending human acts: who, what, where, by what aids, why, how, and when (*S.T.,* I–II, q. 7, a. 3). *Why* entails the reason for the act (*finis operis*), not the agent's motive for the act (*finis operantis*).

67. W. D. Ross, *The Right and the Good* (Oxford: Clarendon Press, 1965), 18–36.

68. Walter, "The Foundation and Formulation of Norms," 132.

69. Ibid.

70. For discussions on the criteria for determining whether or not a proportionate reason exists, see Walter, "The Foundation and Formulation of Norms," 125–54; and Hoose, *Proportionalism,* 81–91.

71. *S.T.,* II–II, q. 47, a. 6.

72. See Ed Vacek, S.J., "Proportionalism: One View of the Debate," *Theological Studies* 46 (1985), 304.

73. See *S.T.,* I–II, q. 94, a. 4.

74. Jean Porter, "Basic Goods and the Human Good in Recent Catholic Moral Theology," 44.

75. Grisez and Boyle, "Response to Our Critics and Collaborators," in Robert P. George, ed., *Natural Law and Moral Inquiry,* 219.

76. Ibid., 231.

77. Pope John Paul II, *Veritatis Splendor* (Vatican City: Libreria Editrice Vaticana, 1993), pars. 71–83.

78. Grisez has challenged the magisterium's teaching on the morality of capital punishment (*CMP,* 219–22; *LCL,* 891–94), but subjects his position to the authority of the magisterium (see *CMP,* 299). Recently, however, the magisterium has refined its teaching that virtually prohibits

any possibility of a legitimate use of capital punishment (see *Catechism of the Catholic Church: Modifications from the* Editio Typica [Rome: Libreria Editrice Vaticana, 1998], par. 2266 and 2267, 19–20).

79. Grisez, *CMP,* 152; and Grisez, Boyle, and Finnis, *Nuclear Deterrence, Morality and Realism,* 254–60.

80. Grisez, *CMP,* 153 (emphasis deleted).

81. See Grisez, Boyle, and Finnis, *Nuclear Deterrence, Morality and Realism,* 261–67.

82. Grisez, "Against Consequentialism," *The American Journal of Jurisprudence* 23 (1978), 39.

83. Finnis, *Moral Absolutes: Tradition, Revision, and Truth* (Washington, D.C.: Catholic University of America Press, 1991), 53.

84. Grisez, *CMP,* 157.

85. Ibid., 101.

86. Ibid., 156.

87. Hallett, *Greater Good,* 21.

88. See Grisez, Boyle, and Finnis, *Nuclear Deterrence, Morality and Realism,* 260.

89. McCormick, *How Brave a New World?,* 5; and McCormick and Paul Ramsey, eds., *Doing Evil to Achieve Good: Moral Choice in Conflict Situations* (Chicago: Loyola University Press, 1978), 251–52.

90. Hoose, "Basic Goods: Continuing the Debate," *Heythrop Journal* 35 (1994), 58.

91. See Garth Hallett, "The 'Incommensurability of Values'," *Heythrop Journal* 28 (1987), 373–87; Finnis' response, *Moral Absolutes,* 51–54; and Hallett's rejoinder, *Greater Good.* ch. 2.92.
Louis Janssens, "Artificial Insemination: Ethical Considerations," *Louvain Studies* 8 (1980), 3–29 (see chapter two for a discussion of the personalist criterion).

93. McCormick, "Notes on Moral Theology: 1985," *Theological Studies* 47 (1986), 87–88.

94. McCormick, *Notes on Moral Theology: 1981 through 1984,* 136. Grisez responds to McCormick's critique (*CMP,* 168, n. 38), pointing out that McCormick has ignored the distinctions he made in *CMP,* 6, E, and "Against Consequentialism."

95. Grisez, Boyle, and Finnis, *Nuclear Deterrence, Morality and Realism,* 266.

96. See Hallett, *Greater Good,* 23–29.

97. Finnis, *Moral Absolutes,* 53.

98. See Robert P. George, "Liberty Under the Moral Law: On B. Hoose's Critique of the Grisez-Finnis Theory of the Human Good," *Heythrop Journal* 34 (1993), 179, who seems to discount the relevance of "the facts of the situation" in determining what is an appropriate choice of action in a particular situation.

99. Grisez, *CMP,* 258.

100. Ibid., 157.

101. Ibid., 300.

102. Grisez, *LCL,* 406–7.

103. Ibid., 405.

104. Ibid., 891–94.

105. It should be noted that in this statement I am in no way advocating use of the death penalty. It is merely a source for comparison between Grisez's adequate and inadequate views of community, depending upon the ethical issue under analysis.

106. Hoose, "Basic Goods: Continuing the Debate," 62.

107. Grisez, *CMP,* 124. See Hoose, "Basic Goods: Continuing the Debate," 62.

108. Grisez, *LCL,* 407 (emphasis added).

2. Reason, Experience, and Method

1. See *Optatam Totius,* in *Documents,* par. 16.

2. See, for example, *Gaudium et Spes,* in *Documents,* par. 44.

3. Grisez notes that "those wishing to understand and/or criticize the ethical theory insofar as it is the fruit of philosophical collaboration should focus on its articulation in two works…" (*Difficult Moral Questions: The Way of the Lord Jesus, Volume Three* [Quincy IL: Franciscan Press, 1997] 850, n. 438). Those two works are: Grisez, Boyle, and Finnis, *Nuclear Deterrence, Morality and Realism* (Oxford, Clarendon Press, 1987); and id., "Practical Principles, Moral Truth and Ultimate Ends," *American Journal of Jurisprudence* 32 (1987), 99–151. While we do utilize those two works in this chapter, given the BGT's claim that revelation fulfills reason, there should be no intrinsic methodological tension between their philosophical and theological projects. Consequently, we rely extensively upon Grisez's

The Way of the Lord Jesus, Volume One: Christian Moral Principles (Chicago: Franciscan Herald Press, 1983) [hereinafter, *CMP*] and *The Way of the Lord Jesus, Volume Two: Living a Christian Life* (Quincy, IL: Franciscan Herald Press, 1993) [hereinafter, *LCL*], in this philosophical chapter. If, however, as will become evident, the BGT's philosophical project is grounded in reason, whereas its theological project is primarily concerned with defending a particular institutional viewpoint (i.e., the magisterial teachings of the Roman Catholic Church), then there is indeed a tension between the two projects. The possibility that that tension challenges the theological credibility of the BGT will be developed in later chapters.

4. Grisez, *CMP,* 7.

5. Ibid., 10.

6. Grisez, "How to Deal with Theological Dissent," in Charles E. Curran and Richard A. McCormick, S.J., eds., *Readings in Moral Theology No. 6: Dissent in the Church* (New York: Paulist Press, 1988), 459.

7. Aquinas, *S.T.,* I–II, q. 91, a. 2. See Pope John Paul II, *Veritatis Splendor,* par. 43.

8. Rigali, "New Epistemology and the Moralist," *Chicago Studies* 11 (1972), 241.

9. Aquinas, *S.T.,* I–II, q. 91, a. 4 (see also, q. 91, a. 2; q. 94, a. 2; II–II, q. 47, a. 6). See Grisez, *CMP,* 173–75.

10. Aquinas, *S.T.,* I–II, q. 94, a. 2. See Grisez, *CMP,* 178–79.

11. See Richard A. McCormick, S.J, *How Brave a New World?: Dilemmas in Bioethics* (Washington, DC: Georgetown University Press, 1981), 5; McCormick and Paul Ramsey, eds., *Doing Evil to Achieve Good: Moral Choice in Conflict Situations* (Chicago: Loyola University Press, 1978), 251–52.

12. Grisez and Shaw, *Fulfillment in Christ: A Summary of Christian Moral Principles* (Notre Dame, IN: University of Notre Dame Press, 1991), 54.

13. Finnis, *Natural Law and Natural Rights,* 34. For a list and discussion of the basic goods, see Grisez, *CMP,* ch. 5, ques. D.

14. See Aquinas, *S.T.,* I–II, q. 94, a. 2.

15. See Finnis, *Natural Law and Natural Rights,* ch. 2; and Josef Fuchs, S.J., "Natural Law or Naturalistic Fallacy?" in Fuchs, Brian McNeil, trans., *Moral Demands and Personal Obligations* (Washington, DC: Georgetown University Press, 1993), 30–51.

16. According to the BGT, the FPM is formulated thus: "In voluntarily acting for human goods and avoiding what is opposed to them, one ought to choose and otherwise will those and only those possibilities whose willing is compatible with a will toward integral human fulfillment" (Grisez, *CMP,* 184 [emphasis deleted]).

17. Grisez, Boyle, and Finnis, *Nuclear Deterrence, Morality and Realism,* 277.

18. Ibid., 284.

19. Ibid., 281.

20. Grisez claims that the basic goods do not have an independent existence, "as if they were Platonic Ideas" (Grisez and Shaw, *Beyond the New Morality* [Notre Dame, IN: University of Notre Dame Press, 1974], 71). Bernard Hoose challenges this claim, however ("Proportionalists, Deontologists and the Human Good," *Heythrop Journal* 33 [1992], 180; and "Basic Goods: Continuing the Debate," *Heythrop Journal* 35 [1994], 58–63).

21. John Langan, S.J., "Briefer Book Reviews: *Natural Law and Natural Rights.* By John Finnis," *International Philosophical Quarterly* 21 (1981), 218.

22. I am indebted to Jean Porter's critique of the BGT on this point (see "'Direct and 'Indirect'"; and "The Natural Law and the Specificity of Christian Morality: A Survey of Recent Work and an Agenda for Future Research," in Todd Salzman, ed., *Method and Catholic Moral Theology: The Ongoing Reconstruction* [Omaha, NE: Creighton University Press, 1999], 209–29).

23. Grisez, *LCL,* 473.

24. Ibid.

25. Porter, "The Natural Law and the Specificity of Christian Morality," 219–20. See, for example, Grisez, *CMP,* 269. Though Porter does not belong to either school, she has entered into the discussion.

26. Grisez and Boyle, "Response to Our Critics and Our Collaborators," 231.

27. Grisez, *LCL,* 509 (emphasis added).

28. Ibid., 473.

29. Ibid., 509.

30. Ibid., 510, n. 100.

31. Ibid., 508–9.

32. Vacek, "Contraception Again—A Conclusion in Search of Convincing Arguments: One Proportionalist's [Mis?]understanding of a Text," in Robert P. George, ed., *Natural Law and Moral Inquiry,* 57.

33. Porter, "'Direct and 'Indirect,'" 629; see Vacek, "Contraception Again," 60–61.

34. Josef Fuchs, S.J., "Natural Law or Naturalistic Fallacy?" 41.

35. Ibid.

36. Grisez, *CMP,* 182–83.

37. For a helpful explanation and chart of the differences between these two worldviews, see Richard M. Gula, S.S., *Reason Informed by Faith: Foundations of Catholic Morality* (New York: Paulist Press, 1989), 30–36.

38. Grisez, *CMP,* 106.

39. Ibid., 902.

40. Ibid.

41. Ibid.

42. See ibid., ch. 6.

43. Grisez, Boyle, and Finnis, *Nuclear Deterrence, Morality and Realism,* 284.

44. Grisez, *CMP,* 182 (emphasis deleted).

45. Grisez, *CMP,* 106.

46. Ibid., 121 (emphasis deleted).

47. Ibid., 860.

48. Ibid., 183.

49. *Gaudium et Spes,* par. 51.

50. *Schema constitutionis pastoralis de ecclesia in mundo huius temporis: Expensio modorum partis secundae* (Vatican City: Vatican Press, 1965), 37–38.

51. Louis Janssens, "Artificial Insemination: Ethical Considerations," *Louvain Studies* 8 (1980), 5–13.

52. Ibid., 15.

53. Ibid.

54. The BGT recognizes this as well, though it formulates this reality in different terminology. That is, "one cannot act at all without accepting some bad side-effects" (Grisez, Boyle, and Finnis, *Nuclear Deterrence, Morality and Realism,* 292; and Grisez, *CMP,* 298). And, "accepting bad side-effects of one's choices can be wrong if one does so unfairly" (ibid.). It seems that there are close parallels between

revisionism's "premoral disvalues" and the BGT's "side-effects" and the means for justifying either, proportionate reason or fairness.

55. See Garth Hallett, "The 'Incommensurability of Values'," *Heythrop Journal* 28 (1987), 373–87; Finnis's response, *Moral Absolutes*, 51–54; and Hallett's rejoinder, *Greater Good: The Case for Proportionalism* (Washington, DC: Georgetown University Press, 1995), ch. 2.

56. Grisez and Boyle, "Response to Our Critics and Our Collaborators," 231.

57. See Grisez and Boyle, *Life and Death With Liberty and Justice* (Notre Dame, IN: University of Notre Dame Press, 1979), 393. I am indebted to Edward Vacek's insightful article on this distinction ("Contraception Again," 52–53).

58. Vacek, "Contraception Again," 52.

59. Garth Hallett, S.J., *Greater Good,* 3–4.

60. See my *Deontology and Teleology: An Investigation of the Normative Debate in Roman Catholic Moral Theology* (Leuven: Leuven University Press, 1995), 46–94.

61. Broad, *Five Types of Ethical Theory* (London: Routledge and K. Paul, 1967, 9th ed.), 206–7.

62. Grisez, Boyle, and Finnis, *Nuclear Deterrence, Morality and Realism,* 276–77 (emphasis added).

63. Janssens, "Artificial Insemination," 5.

64. John Finnis, *Moral Absolutes* 3; Grisez, Boyle, and Finnis, "Practical Principles, Moral Truth and Ultimate Ends," 101.

65. See above, Introduction. For a discussion of this scenario and the different responses to it developed by revisionism and the BGT, see Hoose, "Proportionalists, Deontologists and the Human Good," 179–91; "Basic Goods: Continuing the Debate," 58–63; Robert P. George, "Liberty Under the Moral Law: B. Hoose's Critique of the Grisez-Finnis Theory of the Human Good," *Heythrop Journal* 34 (1993), 175–82; and Grisez, *LCL,* 406–7.

66. The literature on this distinction is extensive. For a helpful bibliography, see James F. Keenan, *Goodness and Rightness in Thomas Aquinas's* Summa Theologiae (Washington, DC: Georgetown University Press, 1992), 197–202.

67. Grisez, *CMP,* 257.

68. Ibid.

69. Ibid., 257–58.

70. Grisez, *LCL,* 506–19.
71. Grisez, *CMP,* 258.
72. Grisez, *LCL,* 507.
73. Ibid., 267.
74. See *Gaudium et Spes,* pars. 13, 33, 44, 46, 52; and *Lumen Gentium,* par. 37.
75. Grisez, *LCL,* 258.
76. Ibid.
77. Ibid.
78. Ibid., 257.
79. Ibid.
80. Ibid., 258.
81. Ibid., 259–60.
82. Ibid., 260, n. 16. I would qualify Grisez's statement, "no proportionalist holds so simple a theory of value."
83. Broad, *Five Types of Ethical Theory,* 206–7.
84. Salzman, *Deontology and Teleology,* 68–74.
85. See John T. Noonan, "Development in Moral Doctrine," *Theological Studies* 54 (1993), 662–77.
86. Grisez, *LCL,* 259.
87. Grisez, *CMP,* 902.
88. Ibid.
89. Ibid.
90. Ibid.
91. Grisez, *CMP,* 10; and, *LCL,* 260–61.
92. Noonan, "Development in Moral Doctrine," 674–75.
93. For example, see John Giles Milhaven, "Objective Moral Evaluation of Consequences," *Theological Studies* 32 (1971), 421–30.
94. See Gustavo Gutiérrez, *A Theology of Liberation* (Maryknoll, NY: Orbis Books, 1988, 2nd ed.).
95. For an informative text on contemporary feminist thought and its implications for moral theology, see Charles E. Curran, Margaret A. Farley, and Richard A. McCormick, S.J., eds., *Readings in Moral Theology No. 9: Feminist Ethics and the Catholic Moral Tradition* (New York: Paulist Press, 1996).
96. Lisa Sowle Cahill, "Feminist Ethics, Differences, and Common Ground: A Catholic Perspective," in Curran, Farley, and McCormick, eds., *Feminist Ethics and the Catholic Moral Tradition,*

185. See also *Sex, Gender, and Christian Ethics* (Cambridge: Cambridge University Press, 1996) for Cahill's emphasis on experience in developing a credible (sexual) ethic.

97. See *"Ordinatio Sacerdotalis* (Apostolic Letter Reserving Priestly Ordination to Men Alone)," *Origins* (May 22, 1994), 49–52.

98. NCCB, *The Challenge of Peace: God's Promise and Our Response* (Washington, DC: U.S.C.C., 1983); *Economic Justice for All: Pastoral Letter on Catholic Social Teaching and the U.S. Economy* (Washington DC: U.S.C.C., 1986).

99. Grisez, *CMP,* 10–11.

100. Grisez, *LCL,* 387–89.

101. Porter, "Basic Goods and the Human Good in Recent Catholic Moral Theology," 48.

102. *Gaudium et Spes,* par. 44.

103. The majority of this chapter was first published as "The Basic Goods Theory and Revisionism: A Methodological Comparison on the Use of Reason and Experience as Sources of Moral Knowledge," *Heythrop Journal* 42 (2001), 423–50.

3. Scripture and Method

1. *Dei Verbum,* in Walter M. Abbott, S.J., ed., *The Documents of Vatican II* (New York: America Press, 1966) [hereinafter, *Documents*], par. 24, 127.

2. Richard A. McCormick, S.J., *Notes on Moral Theology: 1965 through 1980* (Washington, DC: University Press of America, 1981), 814.

3. This position is espoused by what is commonly known as the "Faith-Ethic" school.

4. It should be noted that when we discuss specifically Christian norms, we are not discussing contextual norms, e.g., a Catholic should participate in the Eucharist on Sunday. Such norms are contextually dependent. Specific norms are those that, in theory, could apply to all Christians regardless of context.

5. Grisez, *CMP,* 609 and 625, n. 12.

6. It must be noted that the BGT's use of fundamental option differs from that of revisionism. See Richard A. McCormick, S.J., *Critical*

Calling: Reflections on Moral Dilemmas Since Vatican II (Washington, DC: Georgetown University Press, 1989), 171–90.

7. Germain Grisez and Russell Shaw, *Fulfillment in Christ,* 318.

8. Grisez, *CMP,* 14–15.

9. Norbert Rigali, S.J., "Christian Morality and Universal Morality: The One and the Many," *Louvain Studies* 19 (1994), 19.

10. Rigali, "On Christian Ethics," *Chicago Studies* 10 (1971), 240.

11. Ibid. See also, Curran, *The Living Tradition of Catholic Moral Theology* (Notre Dame, IN: University of Notre Dame Press, 1992), 177–79; McCormick, *Critical Calling,* 50; and *Notes on Moral Theology: 1965 through 1980,* 430–31.

12. Fuchs, *Natural Law: A Theological Investigation,* Helmut Reckter, S.J., trans. (New York: Sheed and Ward, 1965), 156 (emphasis in original).

13. Grisez, *CMP,* 201, n. 15.

14. Josef Fuchs, S.J., "Is There a Specifically Christian Morality?" in Curran and McCormick, eds., *Readings in Moral Theology No. 2: The Distinctiveness of Christian Ethics* (New York: Paulist Press, 1980), 3–19.

15. See William C. Spohn, *What Are They Saying about Scripture and Ethics?* (New York: Paulist Press, 1995 rev. ed.) ch. 5; "Jesus and Ethics," *Catholic Theological Society of America Proceedings* 49 (1994), 40–57; and "Jesus and Christian Ethics: Notes on Moral Theology 1994," *Theological Studies* 56 (1995), 101–7.

16. Grisez and Boyle, "Response to Our Critics and Our Collaborators," in Robert P. George, ed., *Natural Law and Moral Inquiry: Ethics, Metaphysics, and Politics in the Work of Germain Grisez* (Washington, DC: Georgetown University Press, 1998), 231.

17. Thomas Ogletree, *The Use of Bible in Christian Ethics: A Constructive Essay* (Philadelphia, PA: Fortress, 1983), 15–45. See also, Spohn, *What Are They Saying about Scripture and Ethics?,* 8–20; Bruce C. Birch, *Let Justice Roll Down: The Old Testament, Ethics, and Christian Life* (Louisville: Westminster/John Knox, 1991), 20–21; and Paul Jersild, *Spirit Ethics: Scripture and the Moral Life* (Minneapolis, MN: Fortress Press, 2000), 50–55.

18. Grisez and Shaw, *Fulfillment in Christ,* 5.

19. Grisez, *CMP,* 24.

20. See Spohn, *What Are They Saying about Scripture and Ethics?*; and Gareth Moore, "Some Remarks on the Use of Scripture in *Veritatis Splendor*," in Joe Selling and Jan Jans, eds., *Splendor of Accuracy*, 71–98.

21. Grisez, *CMP*, 628.

22. According to the BGT, the first principle of morality is formulated as follows: "In voluntarily acting for human goods and avoiding what is opposed to them, one ought to choose and otherwise will those and only those possibilities whose willing is compatible with a will toward integral human fulfillment" (*CMP*, 184 [emphasis deleted]).

23. See below.

24. *Dei Verbum*, no. 11; cited in Grisez, *CMP*, 836.

25. Grisez, *CMP*, 836.

26. Ibid. (emphasis omitted).

27. Grisez and Shaw, *Fulfillment in Christ*, 407.

28. Ibid.

29. See Germain Grisez, Joseph Boyle, and John Finnis, *Nuclear Deterrence, Morality and Realism* (Oxford: Clarendon Press, 1987), 276–77. While the BGT claims that it is both deontological and teleological, this claim is only justified on the meta-ethical level. On the level of normative ethics and the formulation and justification of absolute norms, the theory is deontological. See my "The Basic Goods Theory and Revisionism: A Methodological Comparison on the Use of Reason and Experience as Sources of Moral Knowledge," *Heythrop Journal* 42 (2001), 423–50.

30. Spohn, *What Are They Saying about Scripture and Ethics?*, 13–20; and "Morality on the Way to Discipleship: The Use of Scripture in *Veritatis Splendor*," in Michael E. Allsopp and John J. O'Keefe, eds., Veritatis Splendor: *American Responses*, 87–89.

31. Grisez, *CMP*, 628.

32. Norman Perrin and Dennis C. Duling, *The New Testament: An Introduction* (New York: Harcourt Brace Jovanovich, Publishers, 1982, 2nd ed.), 270.

33. Grisez, *CMP*, 122.

34. See ibid., ch. 26.

35. Grisez, *DMQ*, 851, n. 440.

36. Pope John Paul II, *Veritatis Splendor*, no. 13 (emphasis added).

37. In fact, four of the five references to the basic goods in *Veritatis Splendor* that Grisez cites are in the context of discussing, either

directly or indirectly, the existence of moral absolutes. Moreover, the encyclical repeats nearly verbatim Grisez's assertion on absolute norms that are limited to negative prohibitions. "In the case of positive moral precepts, prudence always has the task of verifying that they apply in a specific situation, for example, in view of other duties which may be more important or urgent. But the negative moral precepts, those prohibiting certain concrete actions or kinds of behavior as intrinsically evil, do not allow for any legitimate exception." (no. 67). This concern with absolute norms in the encyclical has led some commentators to conclude that the deontological presuppositions of the church have influenced the selection and interpretation of scriptural texts in the encyclical (Spohn, "Morality on the Way to Discipleship," 99ff.). The same could be concluded with regard to the BGT.

38. For a list and definition of these modes, see Grisez, *CMP,* ch. 8.

39. Grisez, *CMP,* 611 (emphasis omitted).

40. Ibid., 302.

41. Ibid., 304–5.

42. Grisez, *CMP,* 634–52.

43. Grisez and Shaw, *Fulfillment in Christ,* 298–99; and Grisez, *CMP,* 609 and 625, n. 12.

44. Grisez, *CMP,* 606–7.

45. Grisez and Shaw, *Fulfillment in Christ,* 300.

46. There is an inherent tension within the BGT concerning the idea of religion as a basic good and an act of faith that transforms the modes of responsibility into Christian modes of response. According to the first principle of morality, one must always remain "open to" integral human fulfillment, which entails all eight basic goods. Furthermore, the eighth mode of responsibility asserts that "one should not be moved by a stronger desire for one instance of an intelligible good to act for it by choosing to destroy, damage, or impede some other instance of an intelligible good...." (Grisez, *CMP,* 216 [emphasis deleted]). The BGT's support for and endorsement of a particular religious tradition (i.e., the Roman Catholic Christian tradition) implies a hierarchy not only among the basic goods (religion is a higher good than the other basic goods), but also within the basic good of religion. Such an endorsement has profound implications for one's "inclination" toward the other goods. When the BGT moves from philosophical ethics to theological ethics, it loses the "ideality of the [first principle of morality]." As Russell Hittenger notes,

the BGT offers a "natural law ethics of indeterminate openness on the one hand, and on the other hand a theological ethics (purportedly consistent with natural law) that determinately shapes the openness according to a specific and concrete end," thus violating the first principle of morality (*A Critique of the New Natural Law Theory* [Notre Dame, IN: University of Notre Dame Press, 1987], 91).

47. See Spohn, "Jesus and Christian Ethics."

48. Grisez and Shaw, *Fulfillment in Christ,* 252.

49. Grisez, *CMP,* 517; *DMQ,* 851 n. 440, in reference to *Veritatis Splendor,* no. 13, which makes the explicit connection between the goods of human beings and the Ten Commandments affirmed by Jesus that are meant to protect these goods.

50. Grisez, *CMP,* ch. 26.

51. Ibid., 664–66.

52. Ibid.

53. Grisez and Shaw, *Fulfillment in Christ,* 258.

54. See Benedict M. Ashley, O.P., "The Scriptural Basis of Grisez's Revision of Moral Theology," in Robert P. George, ed., *Natural Law and Moral Inquiry,* 40–41. Also, see Josef Fuchs's critique of Grisez's use of scripture to find intrinsically evil acts in 1 Cor 6:9–10 and Rom 3:8 ("Das Problem Todsünde," *Stimmen der Zeit* 212 [1994], 75–86). See also Thomas Kopfensteiner's objection to "crude fundamentalism" in the use of scripture in ethics ("Globalization and the Autonomy of Moral Reasoning: An Essay in Fundamental Moral Theology," *Theological Studies* 54 [1993], 501).

55. *Veritatis Splendor,* no. 20.

56. Spohn, *What Are They Saying about Scripture and Ethics?,* 53.

57. Grisez, *CMP,* 607.

58. Ibid. (emphasis deleted).

59. Grisez and Shaw, *Fulfillment in Christ,* 318.

60. Bruno Schüller, S.J., *Wholly Human: Essays on the Theory and Language of Morality,* Peter Heinegg, trans. (Washington, DC: Georgetown University Press, 1986), 15–42.

61. Curran, *Catholic Moral Tradition Today,* 51–52.

62. *Catechism of the Catholic Church* (Rome: Libreria Editrice Vaticana, 1994).

63. Spohn, *What Are They Saying about Scripture and Ethics?,* 40.

64. Bruno Schüller, S.J., "A Contribution to the Theological Discussion of Natural Law," in Curran and McCormick, S.J., eds., *Readings in Moral Theology No. 7: Natural Law and Theology* (New York: Paulist, 1991), 80.

65. See Curran, *Catholic Moral Tradition Today,* x.

66. Fuchs, *Natural Law,* 6–9.

67. Ibid., 162.

68. Ibid., 155–62.

69. John Paul II, "Jubilee Characteristic: The Purification of Memory," *Origins* 29/40 (March 23, 2000), 648–50. See also, International Theological Commission, "Memory and Reconciliation: The Church and Faults of the Past," *Origins* 29/39 (March 16, 2000), 626–44.

70. For an explanation of these two Christologies, see Karl Rahner, "Two Basic Types of Christology," *Theological Investigations: Volume XIII: Theology, Anthropology, Christology,* David Bourke, trans. (New York: Seabury Press, 1975), 213–23.

71. See Col 1:15–17, Eph 1:9–23, and 1 Cor 8:6 (Fuchs, *Natural Law,* 74).

72. Spohn, *What Are They Saying about Scripture and Ethics?,* 97.

73. Spohn, "Jesus and Christian Ethics," 101.

74. See Schüller, "Christianity and the New Man: The Moral Dimension—Specificity of Christian Ethics," in William J. Kelly, S.J., ed., *Theology and Discovery: Essays in Honor of Karl Rahner, S.J.* (Milwaukee: Marquette University Press, 1980), 307–27; and "The Debate on the Specific Character of a Christian Ethics: Some Remarks," in Curran and McCormick, eds., *The Distinctiveness of Christian Ethics,* 207–33.

75. Fuchs, "Is There a Specifically Christian Morality?". See Grisez's response to Fuchs (*CMP,* 624, n. 8).

76. See Spohn, *What Are They Saying about Scripture and Ethics?,* 49–50.

77. Vincent MacNamara, *Faith and Ethics: Recent Roman Catholicism* (Washington, DC: Georgetown University Press, 1985), 106.

78. Grisez, *CMP,* 624, n. 8.

79. MacNamara, *Faith and Ethics,* 108.

80. Grisez, *CMP,* 666.

81. Louis Janssens, "Artificial Insemination: Ethical Considerations," *Louvain Studies* 8 (1980), 12.

82. Ibid.

83. Rigali, "The Uniqueness and the Distinctiveness of Christian Morality and Ethics," in Charles E. Curran, ed., *Moral Theology: Challenges for the Future: Essays in Honor of Richard A. McCormick, S.J* (New York: Paulist Press, 1990), 87.

84. Grisez and Shaw, *Fulfillment in Christ,* 318.

85. See "The Human Act and Its Moral Evaluation in the Catechism of the Catholic Church: A Critical Analysis," in Michael E. Allsopp, ed., *Ethics and the Catechism of the Catholic Church* (Scranton: University of Scranton Press, 1999), 68–71.

86. Spohn, *What Are They Saying about Scripture and Ethics?,* 108.

87. Ibid., 141, n. 22.

88. Ibid., 55; and Spohn, *Go and Do Likewise: Jesus and Ethics* (New York: Continuum, 1999), ch. 3. See David Tracy, *The Analogical Imagination: Christian Theology and the Culture of Pluralism* (New York: Crossroad, 1981).

89. Ibid., 102.

90. See Spohn, *Go and Do Likewise: Jesus and Ethics.*

91. Spohn, "Jesus and Christian Ethics," 104.

92. Ibid.

93. Ibid., 105.

94. Grisez, *CMP,* esp. 192–94; and Grisez and Boyle, "Response to Our Critics and Our Collaborators," 218.

95. Spohn, "Jesus and Christian Ethics," 105.

96. See Hauerwas, *The Peaceable Kingdom: A Primer in Christian Ethics* (Notre Dame, IN: University of Notre Dame Press, 1983).

97. Grisez and Boyle, "Response to Our Critics and Our Collaborators," 218.

98. "Basic Goods and the Human Good in Recent Catholic Moral Theology," *Thomist* 57 (1993), 48–49.

99. See James J. Walter, "The Foundation and Formulation of Norms," in Charles E. Curran, ed., *Moral Theology: Challenges for the Future,* 144–48.

100. Spohn, "Jesus and Christian Ethics," 102.

101. The majority of this chapter was first published as "The Basic Goods Theory and Revisionism: A Methodological Comparison on the Use of Scripture as a Source of Moral Knowledge," *Louvain Studies* 29 (2001), 117–46.

4. Tradition and Method

1. For a historical account of the evolution of the term *magisterium,* see Yves Congar, O.P., "A Semantic History of the Term 'Magisterium,'" in Charles E. Curran and Richard A. McCormick, S.J., eds., *Readings in Moral Theology No. 3: The Magisterium and Morality* (New York: Paulist Press, 1982), 297–313. While recognizing the recent usage and meaning of this term, we will use it for the sake of discussion even when referring to the teaching authority of the church before the 19th century.

2. Heinrich Denzinger and Adolfus Schönmetzer, S.J., *Enchiridion Symbolorum Definitionum et Declarationum de Rebus Fidei et Morum* (Fribourg: Herder, 1967, 34th ed.) [hereinafter, Denzinger], par. 1839.

3. Francis A. Sullivan, S.J., *Creative Fidelity: Weighing and Interpreting the Documents of the Magisterium* (New York: Paulist Press, 1996), 13–14. See James A. Coriden, Thomas J. Green, and Donald E. Heintschel, eds., *The Code of Canon Law: A Text and Commentary* (New York: Paulist Press, 1985) [hereinafter, *Code of Canon Law*], c. 749, 547.

4. *Lumen Gentium,* in Walter M. Abbott, S.J., ed., *The Documents of Vatican II* (New York: America Press, 1966) [hereinafter, *Documents*], pars. 25, 48.

5. *Code of Canon Law,* 547.

6. Francis A. Sullivan, S.J., *Magisterium: Teaching Authority in the Catholic Church* (New York: Paulist Press, 1983), 154–55.

7. *Lumen Gentium,* in *Documents,* pars. 25, 48, n. 122. See Sullivan, "The 'Secondary Object' of Infallibility," *Theological Studies* 54 (1993), 536–50. Charles E. Curran, *The Catholic Moral Tradition Today: A Synthesis* (Washington, DC: Georgetown University Press, 1999), 224–25, notes that in *Ad Tuendam Fidem* (*Origins* 28 [1998], 113–16), John Paul II seemingly adds a third category of infallible teaching. However, this third category is essentially the same as what theologians refer to as "the secondary object of infallibility."

8. While there is much debate over the translation of the Latin, "*obsequium,*" the official commentary on the *Code of Canon Law* notes, "In the language of *Lumen Gentium* 25, the canon speaks of 'religious respect' as the proper response to what legitimate church authority teaches in matters of faith and morals." It continues, "This is a general guideline which incorporates a healthy respect for and acceptance of sound teaching

in the Church" (548). See B. C. Butler, O.S.B. ("Infallible: *Authenticum: Assensus: Obsequium:* Christian Teaching Authority and the Christian's Response," *Doctrine and Life* 31 [1981], 82–87) and Sullivan (*Magisterium,* 158–61) for their exchange on how this term is to be interpreted.

9. See, for example, *The Critical Calling: Reflections on Moral Dilemmas Since Vatican II* (Washington, D.C.: Georgetown University Press, 1989), 19–21, 34–45, 54–55, 163–69; and "Some Early Reactions to *Veritatis Splendor,*" in Curran and McCormick, eds., *Readings in Moral Theology No. 10: John Paul II and Moral Theology* (New York: Paulist Press, 1998), 28–30.

10. Grisez, *CMP,* 831.

11. This model is clearly reflected in Pius XII's *Humani Generis* (see, for example, Denzinger, 2313–14).

12. McCormick, *Critical Calling,* 40. For a helpful study on *communio* as an ecclesiological model, see Jean-Marie Roger Tillard, O.P., *Church of Churches: The Ecclesiology of Communion,* R.C. De Peaux, trans. (Collegeville, MN: The Liturgical Press, 1992).

13. Grisez and Shaw, *Fulfillment in Christ: A Summary of Christian Moral Principles* (Notre Dame, IN: University of Notre Dame Press, 1991), 130.

14. Grisez, "How to Deal with Theological Dissent," in Curran and McCormick, eds., *Readings in Moral Theology No. 6: Dissent in the Church* (New York: Paulist Press, 1988), 460–61.

15. Grisez, *CMP,* 10. We must note that the phrase "constant and very firm" implies infallible statements. If a moral teaching is infallibly taught, it is understood that neither theologians nor the experiences of the faithful could challenge such a teaching. A moral teaching's infallibility, however, is precisely what is being debated between the two theories.

16. Ibid., 10–11.

17. Ibid., 853.

18. Ibid., 854 (while this assertion is made in the context of the faithful's response to noninfallible teachings, the point is reiterated in the context of Grisez's discussion of radical theological dissent [871]).

19. See Richard R. Gaillardetz, *Teaching with Authority: A Theology of the Magisterium of the Church* (Collegeville, MN: Liturgical Press, 1997), 241–52.

20. *Lumen Gentium,* par. 12.

21. Sullivan, *Creative Fidelity,* 97; and *Magisterium: Teaching Authority in the Catholic Church* (New York: Paulist Press, 1983), 84–99.

22. Grisez, *CMP,* 882–83 (emphasis added).

23. Avery Dulles, S.J., "A Half Century of Ecclesiology," *Theological Studies* 50 (1989), 430–31.

24. Grisez critiques Dulles's revisionist ecclesiology (*CMP,* 894–97). In so doing, he posits that this ecclesiology is untenable because it posits a view of revelation and faith that are inconsistent with church teaching (481–85). His critique, however, is both an oversimplification of Dulles's position and utilizes the very tools of a hierarchical ecclesiology that are being debated.

25. Pius XI, *Quadragesimo Anno,* par. 79. See Joseph A. Komonchak, "Subsidiarity in the Church: The State of the Question," *The Jurist* 48 (1988), 298–349; and John R. Quinn, "The Exercise of the Primacy and the Costly Call to Unity," in Phyllis Zagano and Terrence W. Tilley, eds., *The Exercise of the Primacy: Continuing the Dialogue* (New York: Crossroad Publishing Co., 1998), 21–24.

26. Grisez, "How to Deal with Theological Dissent," 443.

27. Ibid., 456.

28. Ibid., 465.

29. Ibid.

30. Ibid.

31. Ibid.

32. Ibid.

33. Ibid.

34. Synod of Bishops, "A Message to the People of God," *Origins* 15/27 (December 19, 1985), 447–48. Cited in Grisez, "How to Deal with Theological Dissent," 443.

35. Cited in ibid., 444. See also, John Kippley, *Fellowship of Catholic Scholars Newsletter* 8 (September 1985), 9 (cited in McCormick, *Critical Calling,* 25).

36. Grisez, "How to Deal with Theological Dissent," 460.

37. Grisez, *CMP,* 853, 856.

38. Ibid., ch. 35.

39. Ibid., 852 (emphasis omitted).

40. Grisez, "How to Deal with Theological Dissent," 456–57.

41. Denzinger, 2313.

42. For anthologies discussing the encyclical and its misrepresentation of the revisionist position, see *supra,* "Introduction," note 5.

43. See McCormick, *Notes on Moral Theology: 1965 through 1980* (Washington, DC: University Press of America, 1981), 262–66.

44. See John T. Noonan, "Development in Moral Doctrine," *Theological Studies* 54 (1993), 662–77.

45. Curran, *Catholic Moral Tradition Today,* 226.

46. Grisez, *CMP,* 884.

47. *Code of Canon Law,* c. 752 and the commentary, 548.

48. Aquinas, *De Veritate,* q. 17, a. 3. See John Mahoney, *The Making of Moral Theology: A Study of the Roman Catholic Tradition* (Oxford: Clarendon Press, 1987), 192.

49. Pope John Paul II, *Veritatis Splendor,* par. 62; and *The Universal Catechism of the Catholic Church* (Rome: Libreria Editrice Vaticana, 1994), par. 1793.

50. Noonan, "Development in Moral Doctrine."

51. John Paul II, "Jubilee Characteristic: The Purification of Memory," *Origins* 29/40 (March 23, 2000), 648–50. See also, International Theological Commission, "Memory and Reconciliation: The Church and Faults of the Past," *Origins* 29/39 (March 16, 2000), 626–44.

52. *Lumen Gentium,* par. 12.

53. *Gaudium et Spes,* par. 44.

54. McCormick, *Critical Calling,* 103.

55. See Joseph Komonchak, "Authority and Magisterium," in William W. May, ed., *Vatican Authority and American Catholic Dissent: The Curran Case and its Consequences* (New York: Crossroad, 1987), 110–11.

56. William C. Spohn, *What Are They Saying about Scripture and Ethics?* (New York: Paulist Press, 1995 rev. ed.), 13–20; "Morality on the Way to Discipleship: The Use of Scripture in Veritatis Splendor," in Michael E. Allsopp and John J. O'Keefe, eds., *Veritatis Splendor,* 87–89; and *Go and Do Likewise: Jesus and Ethics* (New York: Continuum, 1999).

57. *Lumen Gentium,* par. 25.

58. The following literature traces the genesis and development of this debate. It begins with a paper published by Grisez and John C. Ford, S.J., on the infallibility of the church's teaching on artificial birth control: "Contraception and the Infallibility of the Ordinary Magisterium," *Theological Studies* 39 (1978), 258–312, and continues with

the following works: Francis A. Sullivan, *Magisterium;* Grisez, "Infallibility and Specific Moral Norms: A Review Discussion," *Thomist* 49 (1985), 248–87; Sullivan, "The 'Secondary Object' of Infallibility," *Theological Studies* 54 (1993), 536–50; Grisez, "*Quaestio Disputata:* The Ordinary Magisterium's Infallibility: A Reply to Some New Arguments," *Theological Studies* 55 (1994), 720–32, 737–38; Sullivan, "Reply to Germain Grisez," *Theological Studies* 55 (1994), 732–37; and Sullivan, *Creative Fidelity,* 105–6.

59. Both Grisez and Sullivan recognize that canon 749.3 applies to "defined doctrines." However, based on theological reasons, Sullivan would expand the requirement of "clearly established" to doctrines "infallibly *taught* by the ordinary universal magisterium" ("'Secondary Object'" 549; and Grisez, "The Ordinary Magisterium's Infallibility," 730–31).

60. Grisez, "The Ordinary Magisterium's Infallibility," 732.

61. Sullivan, "Reply to Germain Grisez," 732.

62. "Contraception and the Infallibility of the Ordinary Magisterium," 258–312.

63. Sullivan, "Reply to Germain Grisez," 733.

64. See *Origins* 20/1 (17 May 1990), 7.

65. Sullivan, "Reply to Germain Grisez," 735.

66. Ibid., 736–37.

67. Grisez, "The Ordinary Magisterium's Infallibility," 738. See also, *LCL,* 263–64.

68. Ford and Grisez, "Contraception and the Infallibility of the Ordinary Magisterium," 278–80.

69. Grisez, "The Ordinary Magisterium's Infallibility," 737.

70. Grisez explicitly admits this lack of consensus on the issue of artificial birth control: "For, in view of the silence up to now of virtually all the bishops on the teaching's infallibility, as well as the absence of the consensus among theologians who have dealt with the issue, most of the faithful who lack theological training will be unable to see that this teaching has been proposed infallibly" (ibid., 732).

71. Ibid., 738.

72. Grisez, "How to Deal with Theological Dissent," 454 and 464.

73. Grisez, "The Ordinary Magisterium's Infallibility," 732.

74. Grisez and Ford, "Contraception and the Infallibility of the Ordinary Magisterium," 287.

75. "Moral Truths—Truths of Salvation?" 48–67.

76. Ibid., 52. See also, James F. Keenan, S.J., who has written extensively on the goodness/rightness distinction in moral theology: *Goodness and Rightness in Thomas Aquinas's* Summa Theologiae (Washington, DC: Georgetown University Press, 1992); "Distinguishing Charity as Goodness and Prudence as Rightness: A Key to Thomas's *Secunda Pars,*" *Thomist* 56 (1992), 389–411; and "What is Good and What is Right? A New Distinction in Moral Theology," *Church* 5 (1989), 22–28.

77. Sullivan, *supra,* n. 61; McCormick, *Critical Calling,* 98–99.

78. See McCormick, *Critical Calling,* 96–100, 147–62.

79. *Documents,* 232 (emphasis added), see also, n. 90.

80. Finnis, *Moral Absolutes,* 92.

81. *Documents,* 292, par. 79. See Grisez, "Infallibility and Specific Moral Norms," 274.

82. Aquinas, *S.T.,* I–II, q. 94, aa. 4–5. McCormick, *Critical Calling,* 150–51; and John Mahoney, *Making of Moral Theology,* 189–90.

83. McCormick, *Critical Calling,* 151.

84. Grisez, *CMP,* 268.

85. Ibid., 269.

86. Ibid. (emphasis added).

87. Finnis, *Moral Absolutes,* 90.

88. Ibid., 91. See also, Grisez, *CMP,* 269.

89. See Louis Janssens, "Artificial Insemination: Ethical Considerations," *Louvain Studies* 8 (1980), 3–29.

90. Grisez and Boyle, "Response to Our Critics and Our Collaborators," 231.

91. See, for example, Grisez and Joseph Boyle Jr., *Life and Death With Liberty and Justice* (Notre Dame, IN: University of Notre Dame Press, 1979), 393. See Edward Vacek's response to this assertion ("Contraception Again—A Conclusion in Search of Convincing Arguments: One Proportionalist's [Mis?]Understanding of a Text," in *Natural Law and Moral Inquiry,* 52–53.

92. Grisez and Boyle, "Response to Our Critics and Our Collaborators," 231.

93. See, for example, Mahoney, *Making of Moral Theology,* ch. 5.

94. See above, Chapter 2.

95. Grisez, *CMP,* 257.

96. Sullivan, "'Secondary Object,'" 546.

97. Sullivan, *Magisterium,* 152.

98.   See Grisez, "Infallibility and Specific Moral Norms," 274.

99.   Aquinas, *S.T.,* I–II, q. 100, a. 8, ad 3. See McCormick, *Critical Calling* 150; Mahoney, *Making of Moral Theology,* 190; and Grisez, *CMP,* 268–69.

100.   See Bruno Schüller, S.J., "Die Quellen der Moralität: Zur systematischen Ortung eines alten Lehrstücks der Moraltheologie," *Theologie und Philosophie* 59 (1984), 535–59; Joseph Selling, *"Veritatis Splendor* and the Sources of Morality," *Louvain Studies* 19 (1994), 3–17; "The Fundamental Polarity of Moral Discourse," in Todd Salzman, ed., *Method and Catholic Moral Theology: The Ongoing Reconstruction* (Omaha, NE: Creighton University Press, 1999), 26–37; and my *Deontology and Teleology: An Investigation of the Normative Debate in Roman Catholic Moral Theology* (Leuven: Peeters Press, 1995), 267–503.

101.   Grisez, *CMP,* 258.

102.   Grisez, *DMQ,* 160; and William E. May, "AIDS, Marriage and Condoms," *Ethics and Medics* 13/9 (September 1988), 3–4. For revisionist perspectives on this issue, see James F. Keenan, ed., *Catholic Ethicists on HIV/AIDS Prevention* (Maryknoll, N.Y.: Orbis, 2001).

103.   Grisez, *CMP,* 269.

104.   Grisez and Boyle, "Response to Our Critics and Our Collaborators," 228–29. For Vacek's essay, see "Contraception Again," 50–81.

105.   The majority of this chapter was first published as "The Basic Goods Theory and Revisionism: A Methodological Comparison on the Use of Tradition as a Source of Moral Knowledge," *Studia Moralia* 40 (2002), 171–204.

Index

Old Testament, 93, 94
Optatam Totius, 5, 142n. 9, 151n. 1
People of God, 78, 113, 115, 117, 122
Perrin, Norman, 159n. 32
Physicalism, 69
Pius IX, 126
Pius XI, 166n. 25
Pius XII, 119, 165n. 11
Platonic, 40, 51
Porter, Jean, 35, 52, 54, 77, 108, 141n. 4, 146n. 13, 147n. 42, 149n. 74, 153nn. 22, 25, 154n. 33, 157n. 101
Practical reasoning, 20, 21, 41, 47
Pre-Vatican II, 100, 131
Primary object of infallibility. *See* Infallible
Principle of double effect, 27, 28, 29, 43, 53
Proof-texting, 95
Proportionate reason, 15, 17, 27, 28, 29, 30, 31, 32, 33, 34, 35, 39, 40, 41, 42, 43, 44, 47, 60, 65, 68, 71, 97, 139
Prudence, 34, 35, 41

Quinn, John R., 166n. 25

Rahner, Karl, 162n. 70
Ramsey, Paul, 150n. 89, 152n. 11
Rational judgment, 38, 41
Reason, 6, 9, 10, 11, 13, 14, 15, 16, 17, 18, 19, 21, 22, 23, 25, 27, 28, 29, 30, 31, 32, 33, 34, 35, 39, 40, 41, 42, 43, 44, 45, 47, 48, 49, 50,

57, 60, 65, 68, 69, 71, 79, 80, 81, 82, 83, 84, 85, 90, 93, 96, 97, 99, 100, 101, 102, 103, 109, 115, 119, 120, 133, 139
Relativism, 8
Reproductive technologies, 73, 132
Responsible parenthood, 29, 31, 54, 69, 135
Revelation, 11, 12, 13, 14, 15, 16, 18, 25, 48, 71, 77, 79, 80, 81, 85, 86, 87, 97, 99, 100, 109, 111, 115, 119, 122, 129, 130, 136, 138
Rigali, Norbert, 49, 82, 83, 97, 108, 144n. 33, 152n. 8, 158nn. 9, 10, 163n. 83
Rightness/wrongness, 131, 132
  Moral rightness, 30, 130, 131
  Rightness, 7, 27, 30, 32, 33, 34, 44, 47, 61, 63, 64, 65, 109, 130, 131, 132, 133, 134, 136
  Wrongness, 7, 27, 30, 32, 33, 34, 44, 47, 61, 63, 64, 65, 109, 131, 132, 133, 134, 136
Rodger, P. C., 144n. 30
Ross, W. D., 33, 149n. 67

Sacraments, 83
  Eucharist, 83
  Reconciliation, 83
Salzman, Todd A., 142n. 13, 156n. 84, 159n. 29, 163n. 85, 170n. 100
Scholarly pneumatology, 123

Other Books in This Series

What are they saying about Papal Primacy?
by J. Michael Miller, C.S.B.
What are they saying about Matthew?
by Donald Senior, C.P.
What are they saying about Matthew's Sermon on the Mount?
by Warren Carter
What are they saying about Luke?
by Mark Allan Powell
What are they saying about Acts?
by Mark Allan Powell
What are they saying about the Ministerial Priesthood?
by Rev. Daniel Donovan
What are they saying about Scripture and Ethics?
(Revised and Expanded Ed.)
by William C. Spohn
What are they saying about Unbelief?
by Michael Paul Gallagher, S.J.
What are they saying about Environmental Ethics?
by Pamela Smith
What are they saying about the Formation of Pauline Churches?
by Richard S. Ascough
What are they saying about the Trinity?
by Anne Hunt
What are they saying about the Formation of Israel?
by John J. McDermott
What are they saying about the Parables?
by David Gowler
What are they saying about Theological Reflection?
by Robert L. Kinast
What are they saying about Paul and the Law?
by Veronica Koperski
What are they saying about the Pastoral Epistles?
by Mark Harding